PROJECT BASED LEARNING
TOOLKIT SERIES

PBL IN THE ELEMENTARY GRADES

Step-by-Step Guidance, Tools and Tips for Standards-Focused K-5 Projects

BIE
BUCK INSTITUTE
FOR EDUCATION

PBL DONE WELL

BUCK INSTITUTE
FOR EDUCATION

About the Buck Institute for Education

Founded in 1987, the Buck Institute for Education works to expand the effective use of Project Based Learning throughout the world. BIE is a mission-driven not-for-profit 501(c)3 organization based in Novato, California, and is a beneficiary of the Leonard and Beryl Buck Trust. BIE has provided PBL professional development services to thousands of educators, curriculum development consulting, and ongoing support for organizations including school districts, state departments of education, foundations, and other partners in the United States and around the world. BIE hosts annual *PBL World* conferences, and offers online resources at its website and online classes at **PBLU.org**. It published the *Project Based Learning Handbook*, and now publishes the *PBL Toolkit Series* of books on how to do PBL. BIE publications have been translated into nine languages.

PBL IN THE ELEMENTARY GRADES

Principal Authors
Sara Hallermann
John Larmer

Secondary Author
John R. Mergendoller, PhD

Published by Buck Institute for Education
18 Commercial Boulevard., Novato, California 94949 USA
bie.org

May 2016: Second Edition.

Cover Photo by John Parodi, of students from Bahia Vista Elementary School, San Rafael, CA participating in *The Shrimp Project*.

Printed by Unicorn Printing Specialists, Novato, California.
Printed on acid-free paper with soy-based ink.
Designed by Pam Scrutton, San Francisco, California.

ISBN: 978-0-9968598-2-0

PROJECT BASED LEARNING
TOOLKIT SERIES

PBL IN THE ELEMENTARY GRADES

Table of Contents

Foreword: About BIE's *PBL Toolkit Series*

You hold in your hands all you need to plan a project — except, of course, your own idea for what it should be about. This book will guide you in finding that idea, then making it work in your classroom with careful planning and skillful execution. This book has been revised in 2016 to reflect BIE's new model of "Gold Standard" PBL.

BIE is publishing the *PBL Toolkit Series* to help teachers and schools do PBL more effectively. Because if it's not done right, or it's done for the wrong reasons ("someone told us to do it"), PBL will either be a waste of time or, worse yet, backfire on a teacher unprepared for its challenges. PBL is not just one more instructional strategy to try. PBL, done well, requires substantial changes in how teachers teach and how schools are organized.

PBL in the Elementary Grades is the second in a series of short books on specific topics related to Project Based Learning. Each *Toolkit* is built around a combination of examples, guidance, and resources. The first book in the series is the *PBL Starter Kit*, which guides middle and high school teachers in planning and managing their first project. The third book is *PBL for 21st Century Success* which guides secondary teachers on teaching the "4 C's" in projects.

More information and help can be found at the Buck Institute for Education's website, **bie.org,** including Project Search and Project Design tools, links to project libraries, and access to an online PBL community where you can ask questions and contribute your ideas about various PBL topics. You can also find downloadable project planning forms, rubrics, student handouts and other tools, plus articles, blogs, and summaries of PBL research. The website has information about BIE's K-12 professional development services and events, and our systemic support services for partner schools and districts. Finally, don't miss the collection of videos of students and teachers planning and doing PBL, which you can access from the BIE website or through BIE's YouTube channel, **youtube.com/biepbl**.

Good luck! Send us your comments about the *PBL in the Elementary Grades* and other BIE resources so we can make them better. Please post comments on our website's forum or email your thoughts — and success stories too — to **info@ bie.org**.

John R. Mergendoller, Ph.D.
Executive Director

Acknowledgements

We could not have written this book without having learned from the many—and rapidly growing number of—educators who have taught us about the effective practice of PBL. We are encouraged by their hard work on behalf of young people. It is impossible to thank them all, but we would like to acknowledge some specific individuals who have given of their time and wisdom.

The following teachers contributed the Spotlight Projects that are highlighted as examples throughout the book: Abbey Flynn, St. Francis School, Goshen, Kentucky; Dana Holstein, Brookview Elementary School, Foster, West Virginia; Laurel McConville, Mission Hill School, Boston; Carolyn Connor and the Maupin School 3rd grade team, Louisville, Kentucky; Laurette Rogers, now at Students and Teachers Restoring a Watershed (STRAW), Novato, California; Gina DeLorenzo, White Hall Elementary School, Fairmont, West Virginia; Aaron Eisberg, Napa Valley Unified School District, California. Thanks for your dedication and collaboration.

As with all BIE products, this book was reviewed by a number of educators. We thank teachers Elizabeth Zirbel, Gina Olabuenaga, Martina Heppner, Jan Bolgla, Angela Loser, and former administrator Berna Ravitz. Lynn Baker at the West Virginia Department of Education and Teresa Dempsey, Ph.D. at the Educational Service Center of Central Ohio provided expert and detailed feedback. A special shout-out goes to a couple of reviewers who gave us all we asked, whenever we asked: BIE National Faculty members John McCarthy and Jennifer Cruz. Two other members of the National Faculty gave us timely advice: Shannon Cannon and Dayna Laur. We also appreciated the quick response to our questions from Lynn Erickson of C & I Consulting. Long-time PBL champion Sylvia Chard provided us with constructive critique that made this a better resource for K-2 teachers. Speaking of critique, we also thank Ron Berger of Expeditionary Learning for allowing us to use his ideas about critique and revision of student work.

Alfred Solis, BIE Director of New Media, contributed much to the technology section of this book, and provided thoughtful answers to random questions and overall moral support. David Ross, BIE Director of Professional Development, was always willing to be a sounding board and reality check. Other BIE staff who helped in many ways are Jason Ravitz, Claire Adams, and Theresa Siliezar.

Sara Hallermann, another member of the BIE National Faculty and one of the primary authors of this book, contributed her vast and varied expertise in elementary education (and more ideas than we could fit!). She worked long and hard throughout the process, and we really appreciate it.

Finally, John Larmer, BIE's Director of Product Development, was the creative force that brought an idea into fruition, by writing, editing, coordinating and bird-dogging. We are grateful for his — and everyone else's — painstaking efforts, and hope this book will make it easier for elementary teachers to use PBL effectively with their students.

Buck Institute for Education
Novato, CA, USA
February 2011

INTRODUCTION

You've heard about Project Based Learning, and you may even have tried it, but perhaps you're wondering... Sure, it sounds good, but is it right for me and my students? Can I do it in today's educational landscape? Can I make sure it's well-designed, so we meet learning goals and don't waste precious time? Our answer to all these questions is "yes"—with some "buts and ifs" we'll explore in this book. By the end, we hope you'll be planning a project and be ready to provide children with a great learning experience!

This chapter contains information about:

- The Purpose of This Book and How to Use It

- Snapshots of K-5 Projects

- What is Project Based Learning?

- Why Use Project Based Learning as a Teaching Method?

- Misconceptions of PBL

- PBL's Effectiveness: What Experience and Research Tells Us

- How PBL Can Fit in an Elementary School Program

- The Role of the Teacher in PBL

The Purpose of This Book and How to Use It

This book is written for K-5 teachers who may be new to Project Based Learning, or who may have tried PBL before but would like to improve their practice. *PBL in the Elementary Grades* is designed to provide easy to read, practical, step-by-step advice about planning and managing a standards-focused project, and some tools to help you do it well. The basic PBL design we describe can work for any academic content area and grade level. This book reflects BIE's model for "Gold Standard" PBL.

How to Use This Book

This book is meant to be used to actually plan a project while you read it. You can make copies of the following three planning forms we provide in the *Useful Stuff* section, or you can use the electronic versions available at **bie.org/tools/useful**. The three planning forms are:

- **Project Design: Overview:** A two-page form for recording a summary of your project

- **Project Design: Student Learning Guide:** A form for analyzing and planning specific instructional supports for the knowledge and skills students will need to be successful in the project

- **Project Calendar:** A form for planning the daily use of time in your project

We encourage you to complete these forms as you go through each chapter — we'll remind you. You'll also see examples of completed forms from our Spotlight Projects.

Some readers might prefer starting with the *Spotlight Projects* chapter, to see a range of real projects in a variety of grade levels and settings. We refer to these projects throughout the book. We've included another sample project to help you get a picture of PBL in action: a fictitious project described in detail as it unfolds in a second grade classroom, *Managing PBL: A Portrait* on page 75.

In each chapter, you'll see the following special features:

TIPS FROM THE **CLASSROOM**

Advice on various topics from experienced PBL teachers.

Special notes to primary grades teachers for using PBL with younger students.

Additional examples, resources, or notes on specific topics.

✳ USE THIS

Reminder that a form, handout, or example can be found in Useful Stuff, near the back of the book.

Snapshots of Projects in K-5

Projects come in many shapes and sizes. Here are some quick glimpses of project work in K-5 classrooms that show how varied PBL can be:

Kindergarteners *learn about food groups and assemble pictures for menus they create to explain a healthy Thanksgiving meal, which they present to parents and other students.*

Fourth graders *study maps and primary source documents as they take the role of Spanish missionaries deciding where to build the 22nd California mission (if there was to be one) and what it might look like.*

A first grader *revises a butterfly drawing for his team until it looks good enough to include in a boxed set of illustrated cards of state wildlife that the class is creating.*

Fifth graders *analyze the pH of soil and water samples while searching for clues to determine sources of pollution in their town.*

Second graders *reflect on why we remember certain events as they prepare to record podcasts of themselves telling a story about an experience, with descriptive details, a logical sequence, and a conclusion.*

Third graders learn heating, cooling, and basic engineering principles while designing nest houses that will keep squirrels warm in the winter and cool in the summer.

First graders learn about the power of wind while designing, building, and testing model sailboats using recycled materials.

Fifth graders learn about urban planning while assessing the aesthetics of the neighborhood around their school, constructing maps that identify positive and negative characteristics, and recommending improvements.

First graders investigate the contents of suitcases filled with diaries, family photographs, artifacts, maps, and architectural drawings. They generate questions to investigate about family life in their local community long ago so they can create a video on the topic.

Third graders email opinion pieces on what they think should be done with vacant land in their community to an economic development agency for feedback before submitting them to a local newspaper.

Kindergarteners make four different kinds of puppets with help from a local theatre company as they plan how to re-tell classic children's stories in a puppet show.

Second graders try to guess how much food, school supplies, or other kinds of items they could buy with 1000 pennies, then create shopping lists and visit local stores and websites to compare prices to prepare for a presentation about where to buy things.

Fourth graders create a blog to publish their writing on the theme of "What It's Like to Be 10" after reading memoirs of childhood by various authors.

A kindergarten class studies local wildlife and observes the life cycle of animals kept in the classroom, as they make a field guide about their county's woodland creatures.

A kindergarten class studies local wildlife and observes the life cycle of animals kept in the classroom, as they make a field guide about their county's woodland creatures.*

Fifth graders take the role of medical school students and try to determine what might be causing a patient's symptoms: a problem in the respiratory or circulatory system.*

Third graders dig deep into the history of their urban neighborhood though interviews, research, and field visits, then create museum exhibits in the school library.*

First graders learn about communities, rules and laws as they help their school develop behavior rules for different parts of the playground and campus, making posters and a video to share with other students.*

Fourth graders decide to save a local endangered species by starting a conservation effort and restoring creek habitats.*

Second graders run a lunchtime pizza business for two days, culminating a study of what work is like, in which they interviewed people at local businesses.*

Fifth graders learn to collect and display data and plot points on a graph as they figure out which cell phone plan is best for their family and prepare a presentation to their parents and classmates.*

Third graders dig deep into the history of their urban neighborhood though interviews, research, and field visits, then create museum exhibits in the school library.

* These last seven projects are described in detail in this book's *Spotlight Projects* chapter.

What is Project Based Learning?

In Project Based Learning, students are pulled through the curriculum by a meaningful question to explore, an engaging real-world problem to solve, or a challenge to design or create something. Before they can accomplish this, students need to inquire into the topic by asking questions and developing their own answers. To demonstrate what they learn, students create high-quality products and present their work to other people. Students often do project work collaboratively in small teams, guided by the teacher.

Although it is easier to define what PBL is *not* (e.g., worksheets disconnected from larger intellectual inquiry), it is more difficult to define what it is... and in one sentence. Here is how we describe it:

> *Project Based Learning is a teaching method in which students gain knowledge and skills by working for an extended period of time to investigate and respond to an engaging and complex question, problem, or challenge.*

A project should be a rigorous learning experience. It is not the dessert you serve students so they can "have fun" or "get a hands-on experience" after a traditional unit of instruction. Instead, a project is the *main course* that organizes the unit. In most cases, it's helpful to actually think of the project *as* the unit. For more on what a project is and is not, see *Misconceptions of PBL* on page 10.

> If you try to rush a project, there isn't enough time to fully include all the essential elements — and students won't learn as much or as well.

The length of a project can vary. Most projects take from 2-4 weeks to complete, assuming students work on them for only part of a day. Some may be longer, as you'll see when you read about our Spotlight Projects. If you try to rush a project, there isn't enough time to fully include all the essential elements listed below — and students won't learn as much or as well.

A project has typical phases, although no two projects are alike. There is a beginning, middle, and end. For a visual representation of these phases in the BIE model of PBL, see the diagram on page 46, "The Flow of a Project."

Projects can take many forms. We use the term "PBL" broadly, including under its umbrella such similar instructional methods as problem-based learning, design challenges, place-based learning, the use of complex case studies and simulations, and guided inquiry. Other writers distinguish these types of learning from Project Based Learning. We believe they share common characteristics and are more alike than different.

A project could be:

- An exploration of a philosophical question, such as "What is a healthy community?"

- An investigation of a historical event or a natural phenomenon

- A problem-solving situation, either real or in a fictitious scenario

- An in-depth examination of a controversial issue

- A challenge to design a physical or computer-based artifact, develop a plan, or produce an event

- A challenge to create a piece of writing, multimedia, or work of art for a particular audience or purpose

Gold Standard PBL:
Essential Project Design Elements

Whatever form a project takes, it should focus on key student learning goals, and it must have these elements to meet our criteria for high-quality PBL:

Challenging Problem or Question: The project is framed by a meaningful problem to solve or a question to answer, at the appropriate level of challenge.

Sustained Inquiry: Students engage in a rigorous, extended process of asking questions, finding resources, and applying information.

Authenticity: The project features real-world context, tasks and tools, quality standards, or impact — or speaks to students' personal concerns, interests, and issues in their lives.

Student Voice & Choice: Students make some decisions about the project, including how they work and what they create.

Reflection: Students and teachers reflect on the effectiveness of their inquiry and project activities, the quality of student work, obstacles and how to overcome them.

Critique & Revision: Students give, receive, and use feedback to improve their process and products.

Public Product: Students make their project work public by displaying and/ or presenting it to people beyond the classroom.

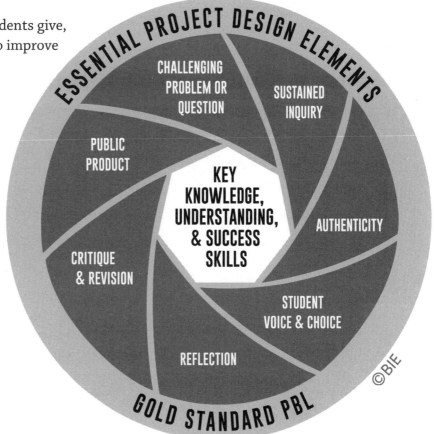

Why Use Project Based Learning as a Teaching Method?

PBL is valuable because it effectively teaches content knowledge and skills, builds deeper understanding of concepts, and makes a school curriculum more engaging and meaningful for students. PBL is one of the best ways to prepare students for the demands of life, citizenship, and work in today's world. To see the research behind these claims, see **bie.org/research**.

An effective way to learn content knowledge and skills

Many critics of the education system in the U.S. and other countries argue that the typical curriculum is "a mile wide and an inch deep." Teachers experience this too, when they have to rush through topics instead of teaching them thoroughly, in order to "cover the standards." And students are aware that they have not learned things well or in depth when they move from unit to unit with no time to be thoughtful or apply what they learn. Students in the upper grades memorize material for test after test — without remembering, the next week, month, or year, very much of what they supposedly "learned."

PBL can help fix this situation. Projects can and should be designed to focus on important content standards — that's one of the main messages of this book. But students taught with PBL are also meant to delve deeply into a topic. They spend time thinking about how to create a complex product or answer a profound question, solve a problem or resolve an issue. In order to successfully complete a project, students still need to gain content knowledge and use academic skills, but they understand concepts more thoroughly and retain what they learn longer.

> If you ask students what they don't like about school, many of them will tell you "it's boring!"

Making a school curriculum more engaging and meaningful

If you ask students what they don't like about school, many of them will tell you "it's boring!"

This is generally less true in the early elementary grades, but even young students may find school work to be less exciting than it could be. Even if a teacher's activities and lessons are not boring and actually fun, students may not see how it connects to anything except the world of school. But in a good project, students readily sense that what they are doing is meaningful. They're working on authentic tasks and products, exploring issues relevant to their lives, and connecting with adults and organizations in the community and beyond. They see how the knowledge and skills they're learning apply to the real world. And some projects — often the most memorable ones — can actually change a young person's life by igniting a lifelong passion for a topic, or by showing them they have the power to do something about what they see in the world.

Building readiness for 21st century work, life, and citizenship

The turn of the 21st century sparked reflection across the nation about the state of our current education system. Three key questions emerged: "How is the world changing?", "What skills and knowledge do our students need to be successful in this new world?" and "How can schools help students develop these skills and knowledge?" *Time* magazine's December 2006 cover story, "How to Bring Our Schools Out of the 20th Century," contained a compelling introduction:

> *There's a dark little joke exchanged by educators with a dissident streak: Rip Van Winkle awakens in the 21st century after a hundred-year snooze and is, of course, utterly bewildered by what he sees. Men and women dash about, talking to small metal devices pinned to their ears. Young people sit at home on sofas, moving miniature athletes around on electronic screens. Older folk defy death and disability with metronomes in their chests and with hips made of metal and plastic. Airports, hospitals, shopping malls — every place Rip goes just baffles him. But when he finally walks into a schoolroom, the old man knows exactly where he is. "This is a school," he declares. "We used to have these back in 1906. Only now the blackboards are green.*

The article exposed the challenge facing America's schools: How can we change the systems originally designed to educate workers for agrarian life and industrial-age factories to systems that prepare students for today's globalized, knowledge-based economy?

The business world tells us that successful employees, managers, entrepreneurs, and leaders in the 21st century economy do not only need knowledge and basic skills like the kind taught in school. They also need to know how to learn new knowledge and skills; to acquire, evaluate and use information from a variety of sources; to work in teams; to solve problems and think critically; to manage complex tasks; and to communicate with a variety of others using a variety of media. These are often called "21st century skills" — we call them "success skills" — and they are being adopted by school systems and states across the U.S. and around the world. But the reality is that many schools have not adopted curriculum design models and instructional methodologies that cultivate these skills. PBL is one of the best ways to be sure these skills are explicitly taught, because well-designed projects require them. (For more on targeting success skills in projects, see page 30.)

> PBL is one of the best ways to be sure success skills are explicitly taught, because well-designed projects require them.

Apart from the demands of the modern workplace, the skills PBL cultivates are useful for life in general. People think critically when they decide what credit card to get, and when they try to find a job. They solve problems big and small, from finding good health care to deciding on the best plants for a garden. They collaborate when coaching a soccer team, or serving on committees of organizations they belong to. They have to handle complicated planning efforts, like parties, weddings, or vacation trips. They communicate to an audience when they write letters, speak in front of a group, and make photo albums as presents. As citizens in a democracy, people need to analyze issues, evaluate sources of information, make decisions and take action, from voting to fundraising to joining (or leading) an effort to make change. All of these competencies — and the desire to use them afterward — can be gained through projects.

Misconceptions of PBL

Many teachers, administrators, parents and the general public have the wrong impression of PBL. They might have gotten that impression from seeing poor examples of it, or from listening to supporters of other instructional methodologies presumed to be in competition with PBL. Some misconceptions about what PBL is, and what it is appropriate for, lead teachers to reject its use in their classroom. However, we think there is a place for PBL in every school, in every grade, and it should be part of the mix of opportunities to learn given to every student.

> We think there is a place for PBL in every school, in every grade, and it should be part of the mix of opportunities to learn given to every student.

Misconception #1

PBL isn't standards-based. It focuses on "soft skills" such as critical thinking and collaboration, but ignores content.

Fact Check: Among PBL practitioners, different models exist and the focus on standards varies. The BIE model for PBL is standards based. Driving Questions are aligned with or even derived from content standards. The major products students create require a demonstration of knowledge and understanding of important concepts, and should be assessed in terms of standards. PBL marries the teaching of critical thinking skills with rich content, because students need something to think critically *about* — it cannot be taught independent of content.

Misconception #2

Young children are not ready for rich content. There isn't enough instructional time for science and social studies-focused projects. We need to teach basic literacy and math skills first.

Fact Check: Knowledge plays an important role in early literacy. To build reading comprehension skills children need to develop broad content knowledge across domains, including science and social studies. In elementary school, content-rich projects build background knowledge that influences comprehension. Additionally, projects can increase student motivation to read, write, and learn mathematics because they are engaged by the topic and have an immediate, meaningful reason to apply these skills. Literacy skills can be taught in the context of a project, especially reading and interpreting non-fiction—an area in which many students typically underperform on standardized tests.

> Projects can increase student motivation to read, write, and learn mathematics because they are engaged by the topic.

Misconception #3

PBL is the same as "making something", "hands-on learning" or "doing an activity."

Fact Check: PBL is often focused on creating physical artifacts, but the artifacts are not as important as the intellectually challenging tasks that led to them. For example, it's not truly PBL if students are *simply* making a collage about a story, constructing a model of the Egyptian pyramids, or analyzing water samples from a lake. These artifacts and activities *could* be part of a rigorous project if they help students meet a complex challenge and address a Driving Question. Some people may also think PBL is like the Montessori method, which is based on self-directed learning, but a project is an extended experience with activities connected by a Driving Question and coached by teachers.

Misconception #4

A project takes too much time.

Fact Check: It is true that projects take time, but it is time well spent. A project is not meant to "cover" a long list of standards, but to teach selected important standards in greater depth. The key is to design a project well, so it aligns with standards, and manage it well, so time is used efficiently.

Note: Some teachers are concerned that *planning* a project takes too much time. PBL does require advance preparation, but it gets easier the more you do it, especially if you can run the same project year after year.

Misconception #5

PBL is only for older students...or fluent English speakers...or those who don't have learning disabilities.

Fact Check: Teachers of all students, from preschool through graduate school, have used PBL effectively. You just have to make adaptations based on your students' needs. For example, first graders will need more direction from the teacher than fourth graders. Doing a project is a natural way to learn, so why deny this to young children? Their inborn sense of curiosity makes inquiry a powerful and engaging learning process. Projects are effective for English Learners because reading and writing is purposeful and connected to personally meaningful experiences. For students with disabilities, use the same support strategies during a project as you would use in other situations, such as differentiation, modeling, and providing more time and scaffolding. Since projects involve more work in small groups, it provides you with better opportunities to meet individual student needs. Finally, projects can provide English Learners and students with disabilities with chances to show their strengths and feel included in the classroom.

Misconception # 6

PBL is too hard to manage, and/or it doesn't fit with my teaching style.

Fact Check: Some teachers find project work to be "messy"—they aren't in total control of their students' every step during project work. You do need to be comfortable with a certain amount of lively interaction and out-of-their-seats activity in the classroom (or outside of it!). A project is never fully predictable, and can evolve while you're in the middle of it, so you have to be flexible and ready to make adjustments. For teachers only used to direct instruction, it may be challenging at first to manage students working in teams and handle the open-endedness of PBL, but with more experience it gets easier. If you need to conduct a project with more structure or prefer a looser approach, either way is OK. What is important is that students are learning as a result of participating in the project. (For more on this topic, see the *Managing Your Project* chapter of this book.)

> A well-designed and well-implemented project helps students see how school connects to the outside world.

PBL's Effectiveness: What Experience and Research Tells Us

Project Based Learning has had its advocates for many years, and more and more teachers and schools in the 21st century are recognizing its value.

Classroom teachers, based on their experience, say that a well-designed and well-implemented project:

- Can work for all kinds of students, with the right support

- Improves students' motivation to learn

- Can be used to teach academic content standards

- Is one of the best ways to build skills such as critical thinking, collaboration, and communication

- Can include multiple opportunities to integrate technology

- Helps students see how school connects to the outside world by making learning relevant and meaningful

- Promotes greater civic participation and global awareness

> Well-designed and well-implemented PBL can improve students' retention of knowledge over time.

Researchers have found that well-designed and well-implemented PBL can:

- Be more effective than traditional instruction in increasing academic achievement

- Increase student engagement in learning

- Improve students' retention of knowledge over time

- Improve students' mastery of success skills

- Be effective in improving the performance of lower-achieving students

- Increase students' achievement on state-administered, standardized tests

Research studies documenting the above claims can be found on the BIE website at **bie.org/research**.

Researchers also would say, naturally, that PBL needs more research, because it has been hard to pin down — so much depends on how it is defined, the particular circumstances in a school, and the quality of classroom implementation.

Schools have used PBL effectively in all grade levels and subjects, and for these special purposes:

- Integrating two or more school subjects and encouraging team teaching

- Providing children with opportunities to interact with adults and the world outside of school and their local community

- Connecting the school to other schools, the community, businesses, and other organizations

How PBL Can Fit in an Elementary School's Literacy Program

To teach reading, writing, oral language skills, and literature, most elementary schools today use a literacy model, some of which must be followed strictly—"with fidelity," as they say—in order to achieve the results promised. One of the requirements is that a certain number of minutes per day must be dedicated to the model. Other literacy programs are more flexible, allowing room for teachers to add their own pieces or combine it with other instructional strategies. The same is true for teaching mathematics; there are strict programs and more flexible ones. Where does PBL fit in all this?

PBL is a flexible teaching methodology that can be part of a school program with any literacy model, but to varying extent:

1. **Fully integrated PBL: Projects are used throughout the school day and program, and may incorporate all content areas, including literacy and math.**

   On one end of the spectrum are schools that use PBL as a vehicle to teach all academic content areas, including literacy and math. Students may do project work throughout the entire day. Schools utilizing this approach would likely have a balanced literacy framework—one that emphasizes the teacher's role in choosing strategies and materials—instead of a scripted commercial reading program. Projects often focus on social studies or science, but may also focus on literature and math, and integrate the arts. Math is usually taught during a protected block of time, although the math skills needed for the project may be included. Literacy is taught within the context of the project, for example:

   ▶ Readers' and Writers' workshops connect to project work

   ▶ Students read to gain knowledge needed for the project

   ▶ Students write to describe learning experiences, create products, and reflect on project work

2. **Partially integrated PBL: Projects occur mainly during the time of day used for science and/or social studies and the arts, but include some literacy and math when appropriate.**

   In the middle, which is where most of the Spotlight Projects in this book fall, are schools where teachers anchor their projects mainly in science or social studies but integrate the arts, literacy and math when appropriate. Teachers in these schools may also design occasional projects that focus on literature or applied math, as long as they are still following the guidelines of their literacy model. Schools utilizing this approach to PBL often use a state or district-adopted literacy program. Math is usually taught as a stand-alone subject, although some applications of math may be included in projects. Students primarily do project work in the afternoon, but some project work is incorporated into the morning literacy block, for example:

▸ Fiction and non-fiction texts that connect to the topic for the project are incorporated into guided reading

▸ Teachers use read-alouds that connect to the project topic

▸ Students write about their research and work on written products during writers' workshop

▸ "Working with words" or academic vocabulary words connect to the project topic

▸ Literature circle texts connect to the project topic

3. **Separate PBL: Projects occur only during separate times of the day/ week and do not connect to the literacy or math programs.**

On the other end of the spectrum, teachers in some schools only conduct projects unconnected to the literacy and math program. Project work is only done in the time in the afternoon when science, social studies, and the arts are taught. Fewer projects may be conducted during the year-perhaps only one or two (which is better than none!). Schools using this approach to PBL typically use a state or district-adopted literacy program that must be followed with fidelity. Math is usually taught as a stand-alone subject, although some applications of math may be included in projects.

Response to Intervention and PBL: Compatible!

There is no reason not to use PBL if your school also uses RtI. All RtI plans require some form of differentiation for struggling students, and projects are flexible enough to allow for it.

One caveat, though: watch out for "new initiative overload" if too many programs are introduced at the same time. Both PBL and RtI require a serious effort, so it would be wise to get a handle on one before starting the other.

The Role of the Teacher in PBL

Once teachers feel comfortable with PBL, they usually say they'd "never go back." They see how well it works for their students. Also, they enjoy their new role, since PBL allows a teacher to work more closely with students, acting more like a coach instead of the "deliverer of knowledge."

If you're used to — and maybe even enjoy — being the center of attention in your classroom and directing the children's every move, you may think PBL is not for you. But although you do need to give up some control and allow students to make choices and create their own questions and products, conducting a project may not be as big a change as you imagine. You still will be the focus much of the time. You're the "project manager" and are responsible for teaching the content knowledge and skills students need. You'll be providing structured lessons, facilitating the inquiry process, and guiding students through the process of creating products. Doing PBL doesn't mean giving students free reign to do and learn what they want. With some PBL experience, your students should be more able to work somewhat independently, but you play a vital role in framing the experience through careful planning, facilitating the inquiry process, assessing learning, and managing logistics.

> PBL allows a teacher to work more closely with students, acting more like a coach instead of the "deliverer of knowledge."

If you teach younger children, you definitely will need to work more closely with them during projects compared to teachers of students in the upper elementary grades. And remember, in PBL you can still perform your main job of teaching basic reading, writing, and math skills. PBL motivates and provides opportunities for children to learn many things, but it is NOT intended to be a "time out" from teaching the basics.

If teaching with PBL feels challenging at first, be assured that your skills will improve over time, as you learn from each project. We'll say more about your role in the chapters that follow, as it relates to specific steps along the way toward planning and managing a successful project. *Managing PBL: A Portrait* on page 75 will also give you a clear example of the role of the teacher in PBL.

 **Bulletin Board**

PBL Prepares Students for 21st Century Challenges

"Let's be clear — we are failing too many of our children. We're sending them into a 21st century economy by sending them through the doors of 20th century schools."

—*Barack Obama*
in a speech at the Center for American Progress

Lots of people are saying the same thing: teaching and learning have to be different in today's world. Education leaders, business leaders, academics and the authors below sound a similar note:

"How has the world of the child changed in the last 150 years? It's hard to imagine any way in which it hasn't changed. They're immersed in all kinds of stuff that was unheard of 150 years ago. And yet, if you look at schools today...they are more similar than dissimilar."

—*Peter Senge*
Director, Center for Organizational Learning, MIT

"Nations around the world are reforming their school systems...to support the more complex knowledge and skills needed in the 21st century, skills needed for framing problems, seeking and organizing information and resources, and working strategically with others to manage and address dilemmas and create new products."

—*Linda Darling-Hammond*, *Powerful Learning*

"One key competency that employers across-the-board value in employees is the ability to think creatively and logically in order to solve problems. Such employees are most likely to be promoted in an unforgiving global economy that requires flexibility and an ability to think, speak, and write logically, to solve problems, and to synthesize information."

—*The American Diplomacy Project*

"Current formal education still prepares students primarily for the world of the past, rather than for possible worlds of the future."

—*Howard Gardner*, *Five Minds for the Future*

GETTING STARTED

This Chapter's Goal

It's time to begin creating your project. You may make the "big picture" decisions described in this chapter in any order. Many teachers start by envisioning what students will do and create as they explore a topic. Others may start with their required content standards and see which ones look like possible candidates for projects. Wherever you start, by the end of this chapter you'll have begun the planning process by:

- Developing an Idea for the Project

- Deciding on the Scope of the Project

- Focusing the Project on Content Standards and Success Skills

- Deciding What Major Products Will be Created and How They Will be Presented

- Writing a Driving Question

✳USE THIS PROJECT PLANNING FORMS

To keep track of the project you create as you read this book, make a copy of the planning forms we provide in the *Useful Stuff* section on page 127-131. Or use an electronic version of these forms, available at **bie.org/tools/useful**.

Developing an Idea for the Project

Don't worry if you've started reading this without having a brilliant idea for a project already in your head. Ideas for projects can come from many sources. Many teachers like to create their own projects from scratch, or you can adapt ideas that have been developed by others.

When you sit and stare at that blank screen or sheet of paper, or when you're ready to begin a brainstorming session with colleagues, you can start from several places. Although many teachers these days look first at their content standards, there's no one best place — it's whatever fits your style and whatever works.

Remember what we said in the *Introduction* about PBL in elementary school: it often makes sense to *anchor your project in science or social studies*. This is especially true if, like most elementary schools today, your school has a literacy and/or math program that does not leave much room for projects — or even other subjects. Planning projects that focus mainly on science or social studies is a great way to put those subjects back in the elementary school day. You can include literacy and math in these projects, and/or art and music, as you see in several of our Spotlight Projects.

You also may recall the Essential Project Design Elements we listed in the *Introduction*. We'll state them again here, to guide you as you start to think of ideas. A "Gold Standard" project includes these features:

- **Key Knowledge and Understanding.** At its core, the project is focused on teaching students important knowledge and skills, derived from standards and key concepts at the heart of academic subject areas.

- **Success Skills.** Students build skills valuable for today's world, such as critical thinking/problem solving, collaboration, self-management and communication, which are taught and assessed.

- **Challenging Problem or Question.** The project is framed by a meaningful problem to solve or a question to answer, at the appropriate level of challenge.

TIPS FROM THE **CLASSROOM**

Name That Project!

Imagine how thrilled your students would be to hear they were starting a project called "Body Health." Now imagine if they'd be more interested in a project called "Jump for a Healthier You!" Or instead of "The Local Geology Project," how about "This Place Rocks!"

To help engage students, give your project a catchy name. The name is not, of course, the most important feature so if it doesn't come to you quickly don't spend too much time on it now — it may occur to you later.

If you'd like to practice, try giving one or more of the Spotlight Projects in the back of this book a new name that would be appealing to students.

- **Sustained Inquiry:** Students engage in a rigorous, extended process of asking questions, finding resources, and applying information.

- **Authenticity:** The project features real-world context, tasks and tools, quality standards, or impact — or speaks to students' personal concerns, interests, and issues in their lives.

- **Student Voice & Choice:** Students make some decisions about the project, including how they work and what they create.

- **Reflection:** Students and teachers reflect on the effectiveness of their inquiry and project activities, the quality of student work, obstacles and how to overcome them.

- **Critique & Revision:** Students give, receive, and use feedback to improve their process and products.

- **Public Product:** Students make their project work public by displaying and/or presenting it to people beyond the classroom.

Common Kinds of Projects

As we said in the *Introduction*, although they all share the essential elements described above, there are several possible kinds of projects, including:

- An exploration of a philosophical question, such as "What is a healthy community?"

- An investigation of a historical event, time period, or a natural phenomenon

- A problem-solving situation, either real or in a fictitious scenario

- An examination of a controversial issue

- A challenge to design a physical or computer-based artifact, develop a plan, or produce an event

- A challenge to create a piece of writing, multimedia, or work of art

Places to Start the Wheels Turning

The standards for the subjects you teach. Ask yourself, as you read through your standards documents and curriculum guides, "Which are the more complex standards — the ones where students need to show in-depth understanding or apply what they're learning?" Those are the best candidates for projects. For example:

- Science Standard (K): "Students know objects can be described in terms of the material they are made of and their physical properties (e.g., color, size, shape, weight, texture, flexibility, attraction to magnets, floating, sinking)."

Potential project: *To demonstrate the physical properties and characteristics of various materials that everyday objects are made of, Kindergarten students create and host interactive displays for the school's "Science Night" using toys, clothing, and other common objects found in the home.*

- Social Studies Standard (1st grade): "The student understands the concepts of goods and services. The student is expected to: identify examples of goods and services in the home, school, and community; identify ways people exchange goods and services."

Potential project: *Students interview their parents and visit various businesses near the school to find out what and how they buy and sell, make a map showing local business locations, then create and operate a "flea market" in their classroom.*

- Science Standard (2nd grade): "Describe how animals may use plants, or other animals, for food, shelter and nesting."

Potential project: *Students are placed in the role of scientists in a fictitious scenario in which various plant species in a local ecosystem are threatened by pests and disease, and try to predict the effects on the ecosystem if they disappear from it.*

- Math Standard (3rd grade): "Formulate questions that can be addressed with data and collect, organize, and display relevant data to answer them."

Potential project: *Students measure the wind in the field behind their school by designing and building a simple anemometer to answer the question, "Is it windy enough here for a wind turbine to create enough energy to power our classroom?"*

- English/Language Arts Standard (4th grade): "Compare and contrast the treatment of similar themes and topics (e.g., opposition of good and evil) and patterns of events (e.g., the quest) in stories, myths, and traditional literature from different cultures."

Potential project: *Students showcase stories from various cultures with written commentary comparing and contrasting them on website pages they create.*

Is there an issue in your community that merits investigation and might inspire students want to do something about it?

- Social Studies Standard (5th grade): "Draw upon data to describe the experience of immigrant groups."

Potential project: *Students capture the experience of a child immigrating to America by using information gathered from stories, maps, interviews and diaries to write and perform a play.*

Your community. Ask yourself, "Is there an issue in our community that merits investigation and might inspire students to want to do something about it?" These can be the focus of powerful action-oriented projects when aligned with your academic content standards. For example:

- Issue: Students learn that an increasing number of cats — lost or abandoned pets or their offspring — are living in unhealthy, dangerous conditions in vacant lots and in parks.

  Potential project: Students analyze the problems the cats face, investigate the reasons why people abandon their pets, then conduct a campaign to raise awareness and propose ways help the cats.

- Issue: Many community residents are not recycling.

  Potential project: Students analyze numerical data on the extent of recycling and plan and conduct a campaign, including public service announcements, presentations and displays at public places to increase participation in a community recycling program.

TIPS FROM THE CLASSROOM

Get Project Ideas from Current Events

Sometimes an opportunity for a project falls into your lap. A celebratory event, a major news story, or a tragedy might suddenly capture children's hearts and attention. Take advantage of the situation and plan a project that connects to things like the Olympics, an election, a natural disaster, a coal mining incident, or a local event such as the arrival of a celebrity or success of a sports team.

- Issue: A local nature reserve is not drawing many visitors from elementary schools or families with young children.

  Potential project: Students create a field guide for parents, teachers, and children to encourage them to explore the reserve's animal and plant life, geology and caves.

- Issue: Some historic buildings in the community are slated for destruction to make way for redevelopment.

  Potential project: Students decide where they stand in the debate over saving the buildings by analyzing their historic significance and weighing the economic pros and cons of the issue. They create website pages, posters, and presentations for the public and local officials to advocate for their point of view, backed by evidence.

- Issue: Families who are new to the community, especially recent immigrants to the U.S., need to learn more about places such as parks, stores, fire and police stations, hospitals, churches, and transportation.

  Potential project: Students create a map of the community locating and describing various places, to make available and present at Back-to-School Night.

What's relevant and interesting to your students. Ask yourself, are my students interested in particular topics? What might be relevant to their lives? This is good test of how well you know your students. A discussion or interest inventory might be a good way to find out more. These topics, although they need to be aligned with important learning goals, are often the most motivating to students. For example:

- A number of the children in the class are fascinated by cars.

  Potential project: Students learn about motion, friction, and other physical science concepts as they design, test, and improve a model car to go as fast as possible.

- The students play with toys, watch TV programs, and wear clothes that are made in many different countries around the world.

  Potential project: Students create an illustrated, annotated map of the world showing where various products and programs come from, and explain how they get to U.S. consumers.

- We need to find a better way to water the vegetables in our class garden.

  Potential project: Students learn engineering concepts and use math to design a pipeline system that transports water from the roof gutters on the school building to the garden.

TIPS FROM THE **CLASSROOM**

It's fine to build projects based on what you personally value-but be careful

In addition to content standards and success skills, many teachers like to include goals for PBL that spring from their personal interests or teaching philosophy.

For example, a teacher may want to help students develop a sense of their own power to make a difference, or introduce them to the world beyond their immediate community. Projects can be a great way to accomplish these kinds of goals.

If you are passionate about a topic, activity, or issue and can legitimately tie it to your curriculum, great. That creates enthusiasm that can light up a project. But be careful about making a project your own crusade, for example a political or social issue. Some students (and parents) may resent it if they feel like they're being enlisted in someone else's cause.

- The mice kept in our classroom die sometimes. So do our other pets, and animals at the zoo.

  Potential project: Students learn how proper nutrition and the prevention of disease can help prolong an animal's life, then create brochures and make presentations at Open House to explain to families what they can do.

- It's too wild at recess. Some children are getting hurt.

  Potential project: Students research, practice, and write instructions for safe games that children can play at recess.

What people do in the world outside of school. Ask yourself, what problems or challenges are faced by people in business and industry, the arts, agriculture, services, professions, or government? For example:

- Farmers grow crops based on climate, soil, resources needed, and economics.

  Potential project: Students study the requirements for successful plant growth as they plan, plant, and grow an organic garden.

- Construction workers and contractors plan how to efficiently build houses and apartments.

  Potential project: Students apply arithmetic skills as they decide how to sequence the steps and assemble the materials when they are needed as they build a cardboard playhouse in their classroom.

- Civil engineers design bridges to make them safe.

  Potential project: Students use math and physical science concepts to design their own Popsicle stick bridge, test its strength by suspending weights, and try to increase its strength by modifying the design.

- Dentists take care of teeth and often find that kids aren't flossing regularly.

  Potential project: Students produce a humorous instructional video that teaches children how to floss and take care of their teeth, and upload it to YouTube.

- Entrepreneurs develop and sell services and products.

  Potential project: Students play the role of entrepreneurs and make a proposal for a new business that meets a community need, presenting it to adults playing the role of potential investors.

- Elected officials decide public policy.

  Potential project: Students examine the condition of playground equipment and landscaping in the local park, prepare a report on its condition and lobby their City Council to improve the park.

Finding Ideas from Other Sources

If your brilliant idea battery is running low, another way to jump-start your thinking is to see if other teachers or organizations might have already thought of just the right project for you — or it could be just right, with a few tweaks.

Try these sources:

- **Your colleagues'** file cabinets might contain project ideas — or ideas could be in their heads, if you ask.

- **Online project libraries** have been set up by some states, school districts, school reform networks, and other educational organizations (see *Bulletin Board* on page 27 for some of our favorites).

- **The teacher's edition of your textbook** or other materials from publishers may contain seeds that can grow into projects.

Deciding on the Scope of the Project

Even though it would be nice to plan the most marvelous project on any topic that appealed to you, and then implement it whenever you wished with all the resources imaginable, with students fully up to the challenge — it's not going to happen. Do a reality check. Your context complicates things and may set limits on how ambitious your project is. If you're new to PBL, you might need to scale back grandiose ideas so your first project is a success. Consider the following questions as you develop an idea and decide on the scope of your project:

What requirements do you live with?

- District curriculum maps and/or pacing guides (if the latter are very strict and cover the whole teaching day, PBL may not be possible)

- Time allocations for subject areas

- Required reading lists

- State and local standards and assessments

What time frame do you operate in?

- School/district calendar, including holidays, breaks, special events, and testing

- When you have access to the library, computer lab, or equipment

- If applicable, the availability of community resources and outside-of-school adults

Bulletin Board

Do You Have Your Virtual Library Card?

Looking for ideas for projects? For a one-stop solution, you can use BIE's Project Search tool at bie.org or find links to the following project libraries:

■ West Virginia Department of Education Teach 21 Instructional Guides:
http://wvde.state.wv.us/instructionalguides/
A large selection of K-12 projects, searchable by subject and grade level.

■ The Project Approach:
http://www.projectapproach.org/
An excellent general PBL site, with several primary-grades project examples.

■ The Center for Innovation in Engineering and Science Education Collaborative Projects:
http://www.k12science.org/collabprojs.html
A collection of engineering and science projects.

■ Try Engineering:
www.tryengineering.org
Engineering and science projects for grade 3 and up.

■ Web Inquiry Projects Examples:
http://webinquiry.org/examples.htm
Teacher and student materials for Math, Science, and Humanities projects.

■ International Education and Resource Network (iEARN):
https://iearn.org/cc/space-2
A nonprofit organization emphasizing online projects that connect teachers and students around the world.

- Your colleagues' timetables, if they are involved in your project or want to schedule their own projects that use the same school facilities and equipment

What is your classroom like?

- Do you teach in a bright new high-tech heaven? Does the room have lots of space for group work? If so, great — plan projects to take advantage of it.

- Or do you teach in a small, leaky, thin-walled portable with no windows? Does your room only have two ancient computers, no Internet connection and one dot-matrix printer? Are the desks still bolted to the floor? Don't despair — you can still run very effective projects, but plan them with the constraints in mind.

What resources are available to you?

- What human resources could be tapped to help with your project — other teachers, other adults in the school, parent volunteers, high school students, community organizations, local businesses?

- What material resources do you have access to — facilities, equipment, technology? High school, middle school, or public libraries?

TIPS FROM THE **CLASSROOM**

First Project? Modest is Best

A project that is ambitious in scope might last a month or more. It would involve multiple subjects and complex products, community outreach, presentations to a large public audience, advanced technology...but if this is your first project you don't need to go there yet. You might want to get comfortable with the basics of PBL first.

Here's what we advise for a modest first project:

- 2 weeks in duration

- 1 curricular area of focus (with integrated literacy standards)

- limited complexity and number of student products

- takes place completely in the classroom, does not include trips into the community

Focusing the Project on Content Standards and Success Skills

Your project should be designed to teach students academic content-area knowledge and skills, drawn from your district or state standards. You should also design your project to build a student's ability to think critically, solve problems, collaborate, and communicate. These are often called "success skills" because students need them in order to be prepared for life and work in today's world. Many educators, school districts, and states — and the business community — are now saying these skills must be explicitly taught in school.

On the *Project Design: Overview* planning form you'll see a place to indicate which standards and skills you've targeted for your project.

Selecting Content Standards for Your Project

You may have come up with your project idea by starting from your standards, in which case you're good to go and can skip to the next section. If you got your idea in another way, and did not consult your standards to zero in on the content and skills that students are required to learn, it's now time to align your project with standards.

If your school or district has identified the standards that are most important for your students, often called "Priority Standards," use them as the focus for projects. They are often based on what items appear more frequently on state tests. If Priority Standards have not been identified for you, decide for yourself or with colleagues in your grade level what the priority standards are for the content areas included in the project.

Start the alignment process by deciding on the few standards that are most essential for meeting the goals of the project. Your natural inclination might be to try to include as many standards as possible in the project since your students will be spending so much time on it. But typically, a project should focus on only 1-3 standards from each academic content area to be included, depending on how specifically they are written. If you try to include too many standards, you can't teach them in any depth or assess them adequately. As you become more experienced with PBL you'll find that longer and more ambitious projects, like "The Shrimp Project" in our *Spotlight Projects* chapter, can include more standards.

Curriculum Maps, Unpacked Standards, and Broad Concepts Can Help You Plan Projects

Before the start of a new school year, map your curriculum to prioritize content for projects. Some districts provide documents that outline the sequence in which standards should be addressed. Often, these curriculum guides or scope and sequence documents contain standards that are "unpacked" into discrete skills and pieces of knowledge. You can use this specific guidance to design project products, assessments, and lessons that align closely with the standards.

Drawing on the work of Lynn Erickson, some districts have organized standards under broad concepts, such as interdependence, conflict, and perspective. Projects and Driving Questions can be designed to explicitly explore concepts like this. For example, if students are studying their community's history for a project, frame it with the concept of change and have them think about why and how places change over time.

✳ USE THIS   **EXAMPLE 4TH GRADE CURRICULUM MAP WITH PROJECTS** *(page 152)*

Selecting Success Skills

Three of the most important success skills are communication, collaboration, and critical thinking/problem solving. See the **Bulletin Board** on page 31 for full descriptions of these skills. These skills plus several others are a natural fit with PBL. We believe that these skills should be taught and assessed in a project. It is not enough to assume students are gaining these skills just because you've designed a challenging project. We'll say more about how to teach and assess these skills in the chapters to follow.

If this is your first project, we recommend that you only teach and assess two. One is oral communication (as in making a presentation) because all projects include presenting to a public audience as an essential element. Presentation skills are relatively straightforward to teach and assess, and they are called for in the Common Core State Standards for English Language Arts (see the **Bulletin Board** on page 32). The other skill that is relatively easy to teach and assess is collaboration or working in a team. Many teachers are familiar with group work and cooperative learning, so you may have the basics already in your tool box.

21st Century Success Skills: More than Text Messaging While Driving

Although knowing how to download music or find free apps for your cell phone may sound like vital 21st century skills, many educators and business leaders today are talking about the skills people in the post-industrial economy will need in order to thrive. For more information, check out the Partnership for 21st Century Learning at **p21.org**.

We believe three skills are especially important for success in the 21st century, and that these skills can be taught and assessed in projects:

Collaboration:

- Takes responsibility for the quality and timeliness of his or her own work; uses feedback; stays on task during group work

- Accepts shared responsibility for the work of the group; helps improve the quality of the work and understanding of other members

- Applies or encourages the use of strategies for facilitating discussion and decision-making

- Manages project by identifying and prioritizing goals and tasks, creating time lines, organizing resources, and monitoring progress

- Respects the ideas, opinions, abilities, values, and feelings of other group members

- Works well with diverse group members

- Encourages group cohesion by using conflict management strategies

Communication (when making a presentation):

- Organizes ideas and develops content appropriate to audiences and situations

- Uses effective oral presentation skills

- Creates media/visual aides that enhance content delivery

- Gauges audience reaction and/or understanding and adjusts presentation appropriately

- Responds to questions appropriately

Critical Thinking/Problem Solving:

- Recognizes and defines problems accurately; raises relevant questions and issues, formulating them clearly and precisely

- Gathers pertinent information from a variety of sources; evaluates the quality of information (source, validity, bias)

- Organizes, analyzes, and synthesizes information to develop well-reasoned conclusions and solutions, judging them against relevant criteria

- Considers alternatives; recognizes and assesses assumptions, implications and practical consequences

Common Core State Standards Related to Presentation Skills for K-5

(See complete document at corestandards.org)

College and Career Readiness Standards for English Language Arts: Speaking and Listening: Presentation of Knowledge and Ideas

Continuum from Kindergarten to Fifth Grade

Anchor Standard	Kindergarten	1st	2nd	3rd	4th	5th
4. Present information, findings, and supporting evidence such that listeners can follow the line of reasoning and the organization, development, and style are appropriate to task, purpose, and audience.	Describe familiar people, places, things, and events and, with prompting and support, provide additional detail.	Describe people, places, things, and events with relevant details, expressing ideas and feelings clearly.	Tell a story or recount an experience with appropriate facts and relevant, descriptive details, speaking audibly in coherent sentences.	Report on a topic or text, tell a story, or recount an experience with appropriate facts and relevant, descriptive details, speaking clearly at an understandable pace.	Report on a topic or text, tell a story, or recount an experience in an organized manner, using appropriate facts and relevant, descriptive details to support main ideas or themes; speak clearly at an understandable pace.	Report on a topic or text or present an opinion, sequencing ideas logically and using appropriate facts and relevant, descriptive details to support main ideas or themes; speak clearly at an understandable pace.
5. Make strategic use of digital media and visual displays of data to express information and enhance understanding of presentations.	Add drawings or other visual displays to descriptions as desired to provide additional detail.	Add drawings or other visual displays to descriptions when appropriate to clarify ideas, thoughts, and feelings.	Create audio recordings of stories or poems; add drawings or other visual displays to stories or recounts of experiences when appropriate to clarify ideas, thoughts, and feelings.	Create engaging audio recordings of stories or poems that demonstrate fluid reading at an understandable pace; add visual displays when appropriate to emphasize or enhance certain facts or details.	Add audio recordings and visual displays to presentations when appropriate to enhance the development of main ideas or themes.	Include multimedia components (e.g., graphics, sound) and visual displays in presentations when appropriate to enhance the development of main ideas or themes.
6. Adapt speech to a variety of contexts and communicative tasks, demonstrating command of formal English when indicated or appropriate.	Speak audibly and express thoughts, feelings, and ideas clearly.	Produce complete sentences when appropriate to task and situation.	Produce complete sentences when appropriate to task and situation in order to provide requested detail or clarification.	Speak in complete sentences when appropriate to task and situation in order to provide requested detail or clarification.	Differentiate between contexts that call for formal English (e.g., presenting ideas) and situations where informal discourse is appropriate (e.g., small-group discussion); use formal English when appropriate to task and situation.	Adapt speech to a variety of contexts and tasks, using formal English when appropriate to task and situation.

Teaching students how to think critically and solve problems is more challenging. These are complex skills that cut across several content areas, and most teachers only have experience with instruction that emphasizes factual and procedural knowledge. Assessing critical thinking/problem solving is also challenging, because it not readily observable (or "score-able" with an answer key). For more on this topic, see the Assessment section on page 49 in the next chapter, *Planning the Details*.

Other skills might be *encouraged* in your project, but not explicitly taught and assessed — such as creativity or global awareness. If you're ambitious, and it's not your first project, you may wish to add more skills to your list of goals, such as project management, the use of various technological tools, and cross-cultural competence. These are all teachable and assessable. Note that if you want to teach multiple success skills, your project will need to be longer, to build in enough time during the project to practice and assess the skills.

Deciding What Major Products Will Be Created and How They Will Be Presented

You may have already decided the major products students are going to complete in your project when you first developed your idea. Sometimes that's where you start, as in, "My students are going to create a field guide to local wild animals." In other projects, you might start with only a topic or a general idea, e.g., "My students are going to help improve the water quality in the lake," or "We're going to explore what it means to grow up." However firm or fuzzy your ideas are for the major products in your project, the following guidelines will help you make specific decisions about them.

Align major products with standards and use them as assessment tools.

The major products you ask students to create should demonstrate what they have learned. By assessing the quality of the products, you can determine whether students have met your goals in terms of standards and success skills. You might have other assessment strategies in the project — such as written assignments, observations, oral questioning, or tests for older students — but the major products tell a big piece of the story.

Check your English/Language Arts standards — if they specify various writing genres for your grade level, use those as the basis for deciding what written products students will create in projects. For example, the Common Core State Standards for writing in grades 1-5 specify opinion pieces, informational/

Contact the Pros about Authentic Products

If you're not familiar with authentic work products from other fields, talk with people at professional organizations such as engineering societies, the Chamber of Commerce, or labor unions. Or contact local college or technical school instructors or university professors to get ideas for project products than reflect real-world practice.

explanatory text, and narratives. These genres align with products in some of our Spotlight Projects, such as the persuasive letters and informational reports students write in "The Shrimp Project" and the newsletter students write in the "Parkland on Display" project.

Make the major products as authentic as possible.

If you're planning a project in which students play a real-world role, imagine what would really happen in a real-world situation. For example, if students are playing the role of scientists, they would not perform a skit to explain photosynthesis — real scientists would design and conduct an experiment to explore some aspect of the process, and then share their results in a presentation to colleagues and in a written report.

For example, students in the "Creatures in Oldham County" Spotlight Project work like actual scientists by generating questions, searching for answers, documenting their findings in their research notebooks, and presenting their work to an audience. In the "What's With This Guy?" Spotlight Project, the fifth graders diagnosing a patient share their analysis with a panel of doctors in the form of a written report and oral presentation, just as they would if they were students in medical school.

Have individual products and/or assessments in addition to team-created products.

Because individual learning is the most important thing you need to assess, make sure you have plenty of evidence of what each student has learned. If the major product is done by a team, it's difficult to determine who learned what and to what degree. You can assess individuals by using such tools as quizzes, tests, oral interviews, or short written tasks. (For more on assessment, see page 47 in the *Planning the Details* chapter.) Or, if it makes sense in the context of your project, have two major products — one created by a team, one by individuals. For example, in the "Cool with School Rules" Spotlight Project, Dana's first graders made video commercials in teams, while each student created a poster to demonstrate understanding of the concepts underlying the project.

Examples of Authentic Culminating Products

Real-World Role	Real-World Product
Architect or contractor	Plan, drawings or model for a building or site; budget proposal
Businessperson or employee of a company	Business plan; proposal for improving business; set of guidelines for employees; annual report; written and/or oral report to supervisors or investors
Chef	Menu; plan for an event; demonstration of food preparation
Citizen	Letter to media or politician; speech to government body; issue campaign
City Planner	Plan for use of land; proposal for civic improvement
Consultants	Written or oral presentation of recommendations
Doctor or health care worker	Written or oral presentation of recommendations for improving or maintaining health; informational brochure or web page for patients
Engineer	Plan, drawings and/or model for a device, structure, system, etc. or an actual artifact
Farmer	Plan for use of land, crops to grow, animals to raise, resources to use
Historian	Informational booklet; web page; brochure for historic site
Interest group representative	Editorial; proposal for policy or law; presentation to politician
Lawyer, Judge	Mock trial
Museum curator	Exhibit (or proposal for one)
Scientist	Design for an experiment; written and/or oral report of findings or research; informational booklet; web page; brochure for natural attraction
Teacher	Lesson (or a plan for one)
Tour guide	Plan for a tour (or conduct an actual tour) of a tourist attraction, historic site, natural feature, city, region, or country

Have students present their work to an audience or otherwise make it public.

Presentation of student work to a public audience is a common feature of PBL for several reasons. One reason is straightforward—to give students practice in success skills. A presentation requires oral communication skills, the use of presentation media, and critical thinking when students decide the best way to deliver a message to a particular audience. Another reason is psychological—students generally are more motivated to do high-quality work if they know it will be seen by someone besides their teacher and their usual classmates. Finally, there's a celebratory and public relations reason. After all their hard work in a project, a presentation is a nice opportunity for students (and you and your school) to demonstrate their learning and shine in front of other people and the community.

Whole-Class Projects Work Well

It can be hard to manage teams of younger students if they are all creating their own products. They usually need a lot of guidance, and you can't be everywhere at once! For example, in our "Pizza Shops and the World of Work" Spotlight Project, Laurel's second graders all pitched in on creating and running one restaurant. In "Creatures in Oldham County" the class created one illustrated book, with each student team creating their own chapter about a different animal.

Consider these potential audiences for students:

- *Other students at school.* Your students can make presentations to other students in their classrooms or invite them to yours; display work on campus; present at special events such as assemblies; or publish their writing or other printed material.

- *Other adults at school.* Invite administrators, other teachers, and other staff members into your classroom.

- *Other adults who visit the school.* When appropriate for your project, and you and your students are ready, invite parents, school district personnel or board members, experts, teachers and parents from other nearby schools, community members, businesspeople, or representatives of local organizations and government.

- *People in the community or online.* Your project can culminate with students presenting or displaying work off campus to community groups, businesses, government bodies, or other schools—or more distant audiences could be reached using video conferencing or webinars. Instead of presenting in person, students can post their work online and discuss it with readers of a blog or solicit feedback from visitors to a website. (For specific ideas and tools for presenting student work online, see the "Using Technology in Your Project" section on page 55 of the next chapter, *Planning the Details*.)

Writing a Driving Question

A project without a Driving Question is like an essay without a thesis. Without one, a reader might be able to pick out the main point a writer is trying to make, but with a thesis the main point of the essay is unmistakable. Without a Driving Question (DQ), students may not understand why they are doing the project. They know that the series of assigned activities or assignments has some connection with a theme, a time period, a place, or concept — but if you ask, "Why are you doing these activities or assignments?" they might answer:

"Because the teacher told us to."

"Because we're doing a project about _____ (neighborhoods; the American Revolution; patterns; seasons; whatever)."

"I don't know."

A Driving Question organizes all the various activities in a project by stating its purpose. The DQ operationalizes the Essential Project Design Element "Challenging Problem or Question."

For students, the Driving Question captures the heart of the project in clear and compelling language, giving them a springboard and direction.

For you as the teacher, the Driving Question is important too. It helps you maintain consistency, guiding you in planning the lessons, resources, and activities that will help students answer it.

Characteristics of a Driving Question

When you write your Driving Question, ask yourself these questions to make sure it's good to go:

1. **Will my students understand it? Will they find it interesting?**

   It might sound good to you, but will kids think it "sounds like a teacher"? Are the concepts and vocabulary appropriate for students in your grade level? Does it capture a topic or present a challenge in an interesting way? For example, instead of "What adaptations do animal species make in order to survive in various habitats?" make it "Could a dog live in the desert?"

2. **Does it require in-depth inquiry and higher-level thinking to answer it? Is it open-ended — are there several possible "right answers" or ways to do the task?**

Here's a good way to test this one: ask yourself, could my students find the answer by Googling it? Students are used to answering simple factual questions in school, but PBL is different. It should take some time and thought to respond to the DQ. Even if the answer is a "yes" or "no" it should be followed by "because…" with a complex explanation. For example, instead of "What are the major industries in our state?" make it "Why does our state produce the things it does?" because that requires a complex answer. Or instead of, "What trees grow in our community?" make it, "How can we create a field guide to trees in our community?" because there's more than one way to design such a product and it requires complex thinking about the purpose and audience.

3. **To answer it, will my students need to learn the important content and skills I've targeted?**

Will the process of exploring the DQ and completing the product allow you to teach to key standards in academic content areas? Will students need to use success skills? For example, a question like "What are our favorite things to do for fun?" which students answer by making a paper collage is not likely to require students to gain new knowledge in any content area or build important new skills. You don't need to actually state the content and skills in the question. For example, instead of "How can we use measurement skills and knowledge of geometry to plan a playground?" you can just say, "How can we plan a good playground?" because in order to do that task, you know students will need to learn about measurement and geometry.

All Driving Questions should communicate the project's purpose.

Examples of Different Ways to Write a Driving Question

All Driving Questions should communicate the project's purpose. With that in mind, you can create your DQ based on your own style and preference, your students' characteristics and interest, and the nature of your project.

There are two basic types of Driving Questions. A DQ can:
1. specify a product to be created, a task to be done, or a problem to solve
2. focus on a philosophical or debatable issue, or an intriguing topic

For each of the two types above, there could be variations. Let's look at some examples, to open up your thinking about what your project's DQ could be. For each set of examples we've noted some considerations about when and how this type of DQ might be used.

1. **DQs that specify a product to be created, a task to be done or problem to solve:**

The following Driving Questions state a concrete goal, and some also state the purpose or criteria for the product. This is a straightforward, easy-to-write type of DQ which works especially well with younger students, because it states a very specific, concrete task.

▶ *How can we create a picture book about the life cycle of animals in Oldham County? (From our Kindergarten Spotlight Project.)*

▶ *How can we make a farm in our classroom?*

▶ *How can we create a web page for other kids that recommends some good books to read?*

▶ *How can we write a historically accurate story about a person who lived in our community long ago?*

TIPS FROM THE CLASSROOM

Use a Template for Writing a Driving Question

To write a Driving Question that specifies a role for students to play and an authentic product they create, you can simply plug the details into this template:

Ask yourself, "Who in the real world does this work?"

Ask yourself, "What products are created or actions taken by the people in this role?"

How can we, as _____ *(role)*, _____ *(do a task/create a product)* **for/to/that** _____ *(purpose & audience)***?**

Ask yourself, "What is the purpose of the product or action — to persuade, inform, propose a solution, be used, etc.— and who is the audience?"

For example:

How can we, as *chefs, plan a dinner menu* **to** *show tourists who come to our restaurant what foods are produced in our area***?**

How can we, as *newspaper reporters, write an article* **that** *explains which buildings in our community should be protected as "historic"***?**

- *How can we write a letter to convince our school board of the best way to decrease waste in our lunch room?*
- *How can we make a musical instrument that produces the same set of three different sounds in sequence?*
- *How can we invent a new toy that is safe, not too expensive, and fun for five year olds?*

The following Driving Questions also specify a task to do, problem to solve, or an authentic product to be created, but *give students a role to play in a fictitious scenario.* This type of DQ also works well with younger children, as well as older students who might find it fun to play a real-world role. It's a good way to show students what adults do in various jobs and professions.

- *How can we, as tour guides, plan a tour to show visitors what to see and do in our city?*
- *How can we, as English town elders, decide who will board the ship to the New World and what they should take, so they can be successful colonists?*
- *How can we, as nurses and doctors, decide which patients have emergencies so we can help them quickly?*
- *What artifacts would we choose as museum curators designing an exhibit about the culture of the Lenape Indians of the lower New York area?*
- *How can we, as agricultural research scientists, design an experiment to show the Vice President of Marketing which company's bean seeds grow the fastest?*
- *How can we, as road builders, make a presentation to our boss about where to put a new road so it doesn't harm animal habitats?*

2. **DQs that focus on a philosophical or debatable issue, or an intriguing topic.**

The following Driving Questions focus on an issue or topic that could be very specific, or on a more general, philosophical question — but do not explicitly state a product, task, or problem to solve. Products for this type of DQ are typically a piece of writing, multimedia, and/or an oral presentation that expresses students' answer to the question. This kind of DQ is most often used with older students, but some may be appropriate for younger ones too.

- *Should our playground be changed?*
- *What should be done about the mice in our school building?*
- *Does it matter how much sleep we get?*
- *Should a park, an apartment building, or something else occupy the empty land in our community?*
- *Do animals in stories act and think like real animals do?*

▶ *What does it mean to be a good friend?*

▶ *How do artists express emotions in their work?*

▶ *What are the most important differences between Atlanta today and what it was like in the past?*

▶ *What was life like for our grandparents when they were young?*

▶ *Why did European explorers of the New World risk their lives?*

TIPS FROM THE **CLASSROOM**

Localize and "Charge" Your Driving Question

Students will find a project more engaging if it relates to their own lives and communities and if it gives them a direct "charge" to take action. Keep this in mind when writing your Driving Question, as in the following examples. Note that to answer *each* Driving Question option below, even though the focus shifts a bit, students would still need to learn the same academic content knowledge.

From: What are effective ways to persuade people to change their behavior?

To: *(Localized & Charged)* How can we make the drop-off zone at our school safer?

From: Who makes decisions that affect people in a community?

To: *(Localized)* Who are the leaders in our community?

To: *(Charged)* How can we plan and host a special event to thank the people who are leaders in our community?

From: How does an ecosystem stay balanced?

To: *(Localized)* How balanced are the ecosystems in our region?

To: *(Charged)* What can we do to help protect the forest ecosystem in our county?

Understanding by Design and PBL

Big Ideas, Enduring Understandings, Essential Questions: How do these features of Understanding by Design, by Grant Wiggins and Jay McTighe, fit with PBL? Easily. A project is an effective way to frame the UbD curriculum and instructional concepts with a focused Driving Question for students. For example:

Social Studies:

Big Idea = community

Enduring Understanding = communities are made up of interdependent parts, including people, government, businesses, and organizations

Essential Question = What is a healthy community?

DQ = How can we write stories to show what it means to live in a healthy community?

Science:

Big Idea = the Earth changes over time

Enduring Understanding = the Earth changes because of erosion, volcanoes, continental drift, and shifts in climate

Essential Question = How has the Earth changed?

DQ = What did the place where we live look like a million years ago? (note: project product is to create an online museum exhibit)

As the examples show, the Driving Question sets students up to demonstrate that they understand the concepts.

Note: If you would like to include Big Ideas, Enduring Understandings, and Essential Questions on your Project Planning Form, add a row just below the one for the Driving Question.

Before Moving On to the Next Chapter

If you've been using the *Project Design: Overview* form to record your project plans as you moved through this chapter, you should have filled in this much so far:

PROJECT DESIGN: OVERVIEW			page 1
Name of Project:		**Duration:**	
Subject/Course:	**Teacher(s):**	**Grade Level:**	
Other subject areas to be included, if any:			
Key Knowledge and Understanding (CCSS or other standards)			
Success Skills (to be taught and assessed)	Critical Thinking/Problem Solving	Self-Management	
	Collaboration	Other:	
Project Summary (include student role, issue, problem or challenge, action taken, and purpose/beneficiary)			
Driving Question			
Entry Event			
Products	Individual:	Specific content and competencies to be assessed:	
	Team:	Specific content and competencies to be assessed:	

Let's move on to plan more of your project's details in the next chapter.

PLANNING THE DETAILS

This Chapter's Goal

Now that you've developed an idea for your project and made some big-picture decisions, it's time for the details. On the next page you'll see a diagram showing the general phases a typical project moves through. To plan for each phase, in this chapter we'll take you through:

- Developing a Balanced Assessment Plan, with Rubrics

- Incorporating Literacy in Your Project

- Using Technology in Your Project

- Launching the Project with an Entry Event

- Mapping Out Daily Teaching and Learning Tasks

- Creating a Project Calendar

- Forming Student Teams

- Communicating with Parents

- Finding and Arranging Resources

The Flow of a Project

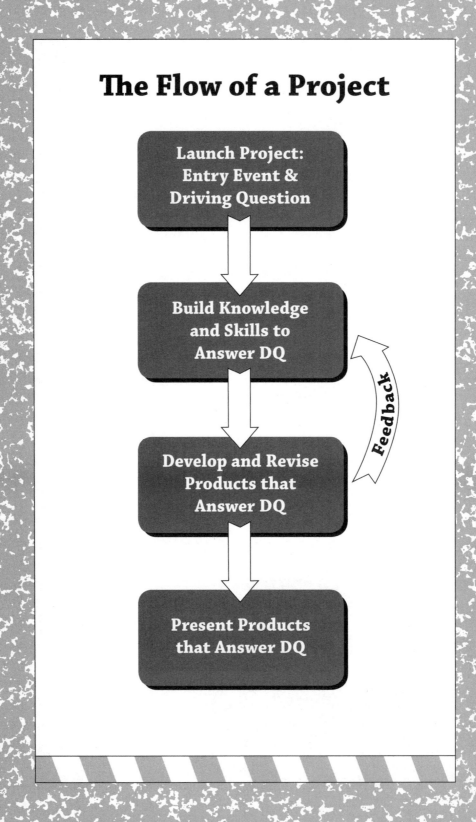

Launch Project:
Entry Event &
Driving Question

Build Knowledge
and Skills to
Answer DQ

Develop and Revise
Products that
Answer DQ

Feedback

Present Products
that Answer DQ

Use of Project Planning Forms as You Go Through this Chapter

As you work through the steps in this chapter, you may continue to record details about your project on the Project Overview form you began to complete in the last chapter.

If you haven't done so already, make copies of the remaining two Project Planning Forms in the back of this book on pages 129-130 or online at **www. bie.org/objects/cat/planning-forms**.

- *Project Design: Student Learning Guide*
- *Project Calendar*

The Flow of a Project

The diagram at left shows the basic phases of a typical project in the BIE model. The relative length of each phase varies — the launch, for example, may take one day or several (see *K-2 How-To* on page 60). This chapter covers three general areas to plan, then guides you through specific things to plan in advance for each phase. In the *Managing Your Project* chapter we'll discuss additional specific strategies to use during each phase.

TIPS FROM THE **CLASSROOM**

Keep Project Materials Together

As you begin to collect materials for your project, including the project planning documents you are creating in this chapter, place all important documents, references, rubrics, assessments, exemplars, etc. in a folder or plastic tub, on your computer, or in a file drawer — or at least in one pile on your desk.

Developing a Balanced Assessment Plan

In traditional education, classroom assessment is done mainly by the teacher. In PBL, students play a bigger role in the assessment process, often evaluating themselves and the work of their peers. Sometimes other adults are involved too, such as when outside experts interact with students and public audiences see their work. In traditional education, factual knowledge and skills such as reading, writing, and using math are typically the focus of assessment. In PBL, success skills such as critical thinking/problem solving, collaboration and communication are also assessed. And traditional assessment practices evaluate only individual learning, not the work produced by a team — in PBL both are assessed. Given all this, an effective PBL teacher needs a well-balanced assessment plan.

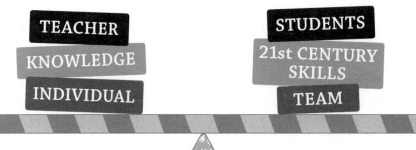

A Well-Balanced Assessment Plan

Assessing Content-Area Knowledge, Skills and Conceptual Understanding

You should still use traditional methods for determining if students are learning the knowledge, skills, and concepts you've targeted in your project. If you teach students in the primary grades, you can observe and listen to students and keep notes on what you see and hear, ask them questions, and look at what they write, draw, and so on. If you teach upper elementary students you can still use, in addition to the above, traditional methods such as writing assignments, quizzes and tests. But in PBL you also assess content knowledge, skills, and conceptual understanding in the products students create and the presentations they make. This needs to be done with the aid of rubrics — we'll say more in a moment about using rubrics in your project.

For example, in our "Cool With School Rules" Spotlight Project, Dana assessed the accurate use of terminology as well as conceptual understanding in the videos her first graders created, and in their oral presentations. She checked to see if they understood the difference between rules and laws, the importance of rules, and other social studies concepts from the standards. In the "Parkland on Display" Spotlight Project, the Maupin Institute's 3rd grade team assessed the students' social studies content knowledge — and their writing skills of course — by reading their biographical sketches of famous residents, walking tour brochures, and newspaper articles. The teachers also looked

TIPS FROM THE **CLASSROOM**

Assess the Important Stuff!

When you assess student work like a poster, museum exhibit, brochure, or PowerPoint slides, put more weight on key learning goals. Usually, content knowledge and conceptual understanding should count for a lot more than how neat the writing is or how colorful it looks. (Unless it's an art project!)

for evidence by examining the student teams' museum exhibits and hearing their presentations. In the "What's With This Guy?" Spotlight Project, Aaron assessed science content knowledge and conceptual understanding when he listened to students presenting their analysis of the patient's disorder and saw their PowerPoint slides, and when they responded to questions from the guest expert.

Bulletin Board ## Prompts for Assessing Critical Thinking

To assess critical thinking skills, the key is to make your students' thought processes transparent. Journals and end-of-project written reflections, or picture diaries and conferences with younger students, can be helpful tools. Create age-appropriate questions that will bring thinking and problem-solving skills to the surface. Use a think-aloud to model how you would respond to prompts such as:

- Give some examples of problems you had to solve in the project and explain how you did it.

- Think back over the project. Were there any choices that you would have made differently? Explain why.

- Did you try different ideas for solving problems or creating _____ (product) in the project? Explain.

- What questions are you asking about the sources of information you are finding as you research your topic?

- What would people with a point of view different from yours say about the issues we're exploring in this project? For example...

- How would you compare what other teams did to what your team did? In what ways was their product, solution and answer to the Driving Question the same or different?

Assessing Success Skills

To assess success skills, use the same approach as you would for a skill like writing. Begin with a clear set of learning goals and decide how students will demonstrate their skills. Teach the skills and give students opportunities to practice. Then assess their skills using more than one piece of evidence.

The following chart shows how a project can provide opportunities for students to demonstrate three of most important success skills, and how a teacher can gather evidence to assess how well they were used. (Note that you can't just provide one opportunity to demonstrate a skill and use one assessment strategy and think that's adequate. It's the combination of experiences, over time and with feedback and reflection — the whole package, so to speak — that effectively builds the skills.)

Assessing Success Skills

Success Skill	Opportunities for Students to Demonstrate the Skill in a Project	How to Assess the Skill
Collaboration	Work in teams to conduct inquiry and create major products Give each other feedback on their work-in-progress Share ideas and knowledge with each other Work with adult mentors, experts, or others beyond the classroom	Observe students as they work in teams, using a rubric or checklist Meet with team representatives and ask them to report on their team's use of collaboration skills Have students use a rubric to assess themselves and their teammates Have students write in a journal or tell you how they worked in a team
Critical Thinking/ Problem Solving	Decide what resources to use and what information from them is most useful Apply what they learn in one area to another Evaluate the quality of various solutions to a problem before deciding on one Explain complex ideas in their own words (for example, the water cycle or why we celebrate Independence Day) Think like experts in different disciplines do, for example: ▶ (scientists) Explain how the scientific method could be used to answer a question (e.g., "Do heavy objects fall faster than lightweight objects?") ▶ (historians) Interpret evidence from a primary source document to better understand a historical event ▶ (readers) Find evidence in the text that supports your interpretation of a story	Have students keep a record of the resources they use and explain why some were more valuable than others Talk with students or have them write in a journal to explain how something they are learning connects to something else Have students explain orally, in writing, and/or during a presentation, the various solutions to a problem they considered and why they chose the one they did Ask students questions during a presentation so they have to explain ideas in more depth
Communication (Oral Presentation)	Make presentations	Use a rubric during presentations, and if appropriate have other students and guests/experts also note evidence of skills, orally or in writing

Creating and Using Rubrics

In PBL, assess products and presentations with a set of clearly articulated, specific criteria. A general description of what you expect is not enough to guide students. You need rubrics. A rubric is now a familiar tool for most teachers, because of the need for "performance assessment" of skills that cannot be measured adequately by traditional tests. A rubric is also an essential tool for giving students meaningful feedback and critique, so they can improve the quality of their work.

For older elementary students we recommend a detailed analytic rubric. This type of rubric is usually written in the form of a table that describes what various levels of quality work look like, along several dimensions. For younger students, use a similar but simpler rubric. See the examples of rubrics for collaboration and presentation skills provided in *Useful Stuff*.

RUBRICS FOR COLLABORATION AND PRESENTATION (*pages 132 to 136*)

✳ USE THIS

Key points to remember about rubrics in PBL:

■ Each major product or performance in your project will need its own rubric.

■ Rubrics are not the same as checklists; they serve different purposes. A checklist is for assessing completion, not quality like a rubric does.

■ Assess content knowledge and subject-area skills separately from success skills such as collaboration and presentation, either by having separate rows in one rubric, or if this gets too complicated, by having two or three separate rubrics.

■ Use student-friendly language and show the rubrics to students early in the project to guide their work. Make sure they understand the rubric thoroughly, ideally by comparing it to an exemplar of the kind of work they are supposed to produce. You could also write rubrics with students.

■ Use your rubrics as formative assessment tools and make them part of the teaching and learning process. Guide students in using the rubric to assess where they are along the continuum of performance while working on their products. Teach students how to use the feedback to revise their work.

Preventing Rubric Fatigue

Some teachers use the term "rubric fatigue" to describe the feeling of being overwhelmed by the task of writing multiple rubrics for a project. To avoid this feeling, adopt school-wide rubrics or rubrics for grade level clusters that can be used for a variety of projects. Sample school-wide rubrics include:

- **Rubrics to assess success skills:**
  - ▶ Collaboration rubric
  - ▶ Presentation rubric

- **Rubrics for common project products:**
  - ▶ Research Journal rubric
  - ▶ Writing rubrics for specific genres (report of information, persuasive, etc.)
  - ▶ Rubrics for graphic design, PowerPoint slides, videos

Incorporating Literacy in Your Project

In case you or someone you encounter needs to shift paradigms about literacy and 21st century PBL, we suggest moving...

From: *"We don't have time for projects. We need to teach basic literacy skills first."*

To: *"We must carve out time for projects. Projects create a meaningful reason for students to read and write and they build content knowledge that students need to comprehend texts."*

Well-designed projects serve as vehicles for teaching literacy in the elementary school. Every project, regardless of the subject area focus or the time of day in which most of the teaching occurs, should provide opportunities for children to read a variety of texts to build background knowledge and find answers to their questions. Students should produce at least one well-crafted written product in each project, aligned with the writing genres in grade-level standards. For teachers using the fully integrated PBL model, projects are the main vehicle for teaching literacy. For teachers using a partially integrated or separate PBL model, a Science or Social Studies-focused project can provide a "double dose" of literacy while building content knowledge that influences reading comprehension. As Ron Berger says in his book *An Ethic of Excellence* when he is asked about whether projects can teach basic literacy (and math) skills:

It's not simply that this work entails lots of reading and writing, but that we explicitly teach reading and writing skills formally during the work. Rather than limit the time available for literacy skills, this approach builds in literacy instruction all day long.

If your projects generally happen in the afternoon, help your students see the relationship between what happens during your morning literacy block and your afternoon projects. For example:

■ Model the use of literacy strategies taught during the morning literacy block when incorporating fiction or non-fiction — including materials not commonly found in the classroom such as newspapers, pamphlets, diagrams, and websites — into science or social studies focused projects.

■ Explicitly teach strategies for understanding vocabulary words related to your project using the same vocabulary development strategies used during your literacy block.

■ If you use Writer's Workshop to scaffold the writing process during your literacy block, use a similar process to scaffold the writing process for the key culminating products that are written products.

■ Use literature circles as a structure for reading fiction and non-fiction related to your project. (See the **Tip from the Classroom** on the next page for more on how to do this.)

Our **Spotlight Projects** feature several examples of how literacy is incorporated into project work. In "Pizza and the World of Work" the second graders read stories about people at work (and pizza), and nonfiction text such as restaurant menus and recipes. They summarized written notes from interviews with their families and people who worked in pizza restaurants, and wrote advertisements, menus, job descriptions, and journal entries. In "Parkland on Display" the students learned about their community's history by reading primary source documents and magazine articles. They wrote summaries, newspaper feature articles, museum exhibit captions, and informational reports while practicing how to take notes and refine their writing — all of which addressed important parts of the 3rd grade standards.

Use Literature Circles to Support Inquiry

One way to incorporate literature into your project with older elementary students is through a literature circle, which is like a book club discussion adults might have, but more focused. A variety of formats can work well with PBL, such as the following:

1. Have students remain in their project teams.

2. Select a text that connects to the topic of the project. It may be short or lengthy and may include fiction, non-fiction, poems, articles, or any other text. If teams will be focusing on different sub-topics, transition from general texts into texts that specifically address the topics they are focusing on.

3. Distribute multiple copies of the text to each team.

4. Teach students the procedure for literature circles.

5. Review the Driving Question and ask students to record additional questions they would like to answer in their research notebooks.

6. Have students read and apply literacy strategies while reading. (For example, if you're focusing on the use of sticky notes to record connections or questions while reading, have students apply this strategy.)

7. Have students record answers to their questions and new questions that emerge in their research notebooks.

8. Facilitate discussions of what students find in the text and how it applies to the project and it will help them create products. Continue the reading-recording-discussion cycle until the group is finished with the text.

Using Technology in Your Project

Technology can help students manage their work as well as create and present products, and it can help teachers manage a project.

Technology is not a necessity in PBL. Amazing projects can happen in low-tech classrooms. And if you do include technology, remember that while it is a useful tool, it is not the point of a project. Think of it as a tool for inquiry, communication, collaboration, project management and product development, rather than an end in itself.

That being said, technology can enhance projects in many ways, from the quality of student products to the efficiency of their work. Using laptops, cameras, and online tools can make a project engaging for students. Technology is an integrated part of children's lives today. They are "digital natives." So plan some projects that take advantage of the fact that most children love it. It can motivate students to do high-quality work. They see relevance and find project work meaningful when they use technological tools that are actually used by the professionals who perform similar tasks in the real world.

Use three basic criteria for selecting technological tools.

First, is it easy to use — can students learn to use it quickly, is it intuitive?

Second, will it last — will the website or application be there for a while, with maintenance and support?

Third, is it cost-effective — will you get enough bang for the buck?

Bulletin Board

Technology in the Common Core State Standards

Most experts advocate integrating technology into core academics, rather than teaching technological skills separately. This idea is reflected in the Common Core State Standards for both Mathematics and English Language Arts which emphasize that, in order to be college and career ready, students should know how to:

- Learn skills through technology and multimedia

- Identify the tools that will help perform different tasks

- Use technology as tools to solve problems

- Use technology to create and publish writing

- Use technology to collaborate

- Evaluate information presented in different media and formats

- Create presentations with digital media

Technology for Students

To build students' technology skills and help them manage tasks throughout your project, consider the following ideas. Use your judgment about what young students are capable of using and what's appropriate — and consult your school's policies, of course.

Conducting Inquiry:

- Use **Skype.com** or **Oovoo.com** to video-conference with an expert and allow your students to pose questions. New features in these services will include ways to conference with multiple people, such as a panel of experts.

- Have students use email to submit questions to experts or contact agencies and organizations, under your supervision, or set up a class email account.

- When students use the Internet, guide them in searching for answers to their questions. They will need support in evaluating the validity of information found. (For example, Wikipedia is not always a reliable reference.) The wealth of information posted on the Internet can be overwhelming, even for adults. You may wish to filter the websites students can access, after you've verified which ones will be most useful and appropriate.

Managing Their Work:

- Have students use shared file systems like Google Documents (**docs.google.com**) to put documents online for collaboration on drafts of products, commenting on each other's work, collecting research notes and resources, or keeping and updating a project task list and calendar.

- If they are using Word documents, have students use **Dropbox.com** to collect and store their work during a project. It helps them keep track of multiple drafts, and it's a safe place for documents — they can never be left at home (and the dog can't eat them!).

- Setting up a team Wiki (**Wikispaces.com**) is also a good tool for collecting pieces of work, adding documents, and linking to resources.

- Have students organize and analyze data they collect by using tech applications like spreadsheets or graphing software to help them visualize the results and look at their data in a variety of ways.

TIPS FROM THE CLASSROOM

Use free trial periods to evaluate tech tools

Many online products feature free trial periods of new versions for 30 days. Before making a decision about whether to buy a product, have your students use them (in a 29-day project!).

Creating Products and Presentations:

- Instead of the same old paper posters, use **Glogster.com** to design posters, to post online or print.

- Use **Storybird.com** to collaboratively create books for all ages by assembling images and adding text.

- Go beyond basic PowerPoint slides by having students organize content for presentations in web-based multimedia tools like **Prezi.com** or **VoiceThread.com**, or use **SlideRocket.com** to add an audio track to PowerPoint presentations.

- Create word clouds on **Wordle.net**, to print or display online.

- Use **Edublog.org**, Google Sites (**sites.google.com**), **Kidblog.org**, or **Weebly.com** and **Blogger.com** to create websites where students can exhibit their products or create digital portfolios of work. Older students can create their own websites, or you can create a class website (which you can ask tech-savvy students to manage!).

- Keep project work in a digital portfolio, which can be shared with an audience in a culminating presentation.

- Students can use a growing list of free, user-friendly applications to create multimedia products, often as an authentic alternative to traditional written products. For example:

  - Instead of writing informational reports about events, have students write scripts and record newscasts using video cameras and online video editing programs such as **wevideo.com** or **youtube.com**.

  - Instead of writing descriptive essays about a place, have them create a field guide illustrated with digital images using online publishing tools such as **lulu.com**.

  - Instead of writing how-to paragraphs, have students develop content for a Web page with directions for how to create something, with diagrams and images of the final product.

  - Write reviews on sites like Amazon to complement a book report

  - In addition to writing persuasive essays about a topic, have students write slogans and scripts for Public Service Announcements.

Technology for Teachers

To help you manage your project, consider these ideas:

- To formatively assess your students' content knowledge before you move on during a project, use **PollEverywhere.com** to generate instant responses to questions and prompts.

- Collect and store student work using **Dropbox.com**.

- Use **Edmodo.com** to create, distribute, and assess student assignments, share digital content with students, and connect with other teachers.

- Create pages in your website for project documents.

- To critique your students' draft products, have them submit their work to you and/or to experts for feedback using email or by uploading it to a project blog or wiki.

Bulletin Board Online Collaboratives for Teachers

The following websites are good places to connect with other teachers for collaboration, resources and project idea-sharing:

- **edupln.ning.com**
  (The Educator's Personal Learning Network)

- **globaleducation.ning.com**
  (social network of the Global Education Conference)

- **classroom20.com**
  (for those interested in Web 2.0 and social media in education)

- **cilc.org**
  (Center for Interactive Learning and Collaboration)

If you have a Twitter account, check out:

- **#edchat**
  (general education chat Tuesdays at 7 PM)

- **#elemchat**
  (elementary chat Saturdays at 5 PM)

- Have students use **twitter.com** or **tumblr.com** to give you status updates on the progress of their work.

- Use Google Forms, a tool in the suite of Google Documents, to generate a variety of assessments including short answer and multiple choice questions, and check boxes. You can email the assessment to students and then easily download a summary of their responses.

Launching the Project with an Entry Event

Many teachers might assume that starting a project is like announcing any other big assignment or activity: you describe the basic topic and learning goals, tell students what they'll be doing, give the time frame, and so on. But your students will get more engaged and take ownership of the project if you launch it with an event that grabs their hearts and minds. An Entry Event is like a warm-up to a lesson, in many ways. Or think of an effective movie preview or a sudden invitation to go on a trip with someone — it gets your attention, leads you ask to questions, and makes you want to take further steps. An Entry Event has two basic purposes: to spark student interest and curiosity, and to begin the inquiry process by leading students to ask questions.

Remember what we said in the *Introduction* about how, in PBL, the project is the "main course" not the "dessert"? That means the project is the organizer of curriculum and instruction. It is not an "activity" you do after teaching the material. So your Entry Event should be what starts it all off. It should NOT be preceded by teaching students what they will need to know in terms of project-specific content knowledge. You can warm students up a little by giving them a general preview of the topic, but just enough to focus them. For example, you can say, "We're going to be starting a project about weather. You know, rain, sunshine, snow, wind…." and then start the Entry Event. (For tips on Entry Events with very young students, see the *K-2 How-To* box on the next page.)

The Entry Event can take many forms:

- Have a discussion about an issue of interest or events in the news.
  - ▶ *Students share stories after a recent flood in the area, leading to a project about geography, weather, and climate in which students compare flood risks in different regions of the world.*
  - ▶ *The discovery of mice in the school building leads to a lively discussion about the children's reactions and questions, launching a project to study the animals and recommend actions the school should take, considering the pros and cons of various solutions.*

- Go on a field trip (or even a virtual one, by creating a Google Maps tour).
  - ▶ *Second graders walk to stores, restaurants and other businesses near the school, observing how they sell various goods and services, launching a project in which students create their own in-school stores and services.*
  - ▶ *Students visit a nearby park or natural area and take note of the number of pieces and type of litter they see, which generates interest in taking action to reduce it.*

- Conduct a demonstration or activity.
  - *Children listen to a recording of a story with sound effects, then engage in imaginative play with various artifacts, to introduce a project on the culture of local Native American peoples.*
  - *The class tastes various smoothies and tries to guess what proportion of ingredients was in each one, leading to a project involving fractions and cooking.*

One Entry Event Might Not Do It

A single event to launch a project may not "grab" and focus younger children as quickly as it would older students. They might have no experience with a topic — or interest in it — and have widely varying degrees of prior knowledge. Five, six and seven year olds may not be able to envision themselves creating the product you have in mind, and a presentation three weeks away feels like the distant future.

If you think this is true for your project and your students, let the children explore a topic through some hands-on experience *before* getting into more focused work on a particular product or culminating presentation/activity. It's OK to mention the end goal when you start the project, but re-focus them on that after they've had enough shared experience to understand what you're asking them to do.

For example, if your project was about creating informational signs for a local nature area, start by taking the children there. Let them draw pictures, write, tell stories, and interview each other about their observations. After these experiences, bring in a guest speaker from the nature area to ask for their help in the project. Then get the class started on more focused work on the products and presentations.

Another example: On the first day of our 2nd grade "Pizza and the World of Work" Spotlight Project, teacher Laurel McConville talked about the jobs she had before becoming a teacher. After the children decided they would like to operate their own pizza business, she had them engage in imaginative play for a while. During this time the children explored what it meant to do work and built up their shared knowledge of what was involved in running a pizza business. Then they were ready to tackle the culminating task.

- Give students a piece of correspondence (real or fictitious) presenting a challenge.

  - *(Real) A memo from the principal asks students to plan an "Olympics Day" event for the school.*

  - *(Fictitious) An email message from a local tourism agency asks students, in the role of marketing consultants, to create materials promoting local historic sites.*

- Visit websites.

  - *Students visit websites showing images of innovative new product ideas, leading to a project in which students invent a new product.*

  - *Students visit websites of schools in other countries, generating ideas about how they could exchange information about themselves and their communities.*

- Invite a guest speaker (or video-conference with one).

  - *A retired farmer visits the class to share family artifacts and photos and discuss his early life on a local homestead, leading to an investigation comparing and contrasting life in the community long ago and today.*

  - *The class uses **Skype.com** to hear from a scientist at a nearby university who is studying changing weather patterns in the state, who asks students to collect data for her by constructing and setting up various measuring devices around their school.*

- Show a video or scenes from a film, fictional or documentary.

  - *First graders watch funny scenes from the TV show "Sesame Street" to generate interest in a project in which they create their own videos about phonics.*

  - *Fourth graders watch the film "The Red Jacket," set in the Miao region of China, to build their interest in a project about peasant life in modern China.*

- Read (or listen to a reading of) a provocative piece of text.

  - *The teacher starts a project on geography and habitats by showing a picture of a "Season's Greetings" card showing penguins with reindeer, and reads an email from a customer to the card's manufacturer complaining that the birds actually live only near the South Pole.*

  - *An article about the decline of the local turtle population raises students' concerns, starting a turtle conservation project.*

- Present a startling set of statistics or a puzzling problem

  - *Data showing the rise in obesity rates and other health problems in young people kicks off a project about nutrition.*

  - *Students are presented with a math challenge involving how much fencing would be minimally needed for various plots of ranch land, leading to a measurement project.*

- Display photographs or works of art or play a song
  - *Kindergartners study and sort pictures (in print and online) of mountains, deserts, rivers, oceans, valleys and other local landforms, starting them on a project in which they create and enact stories of animals living in each environment.*
  - *Fifth graders take a gallery walk to view Thomas Nast's pictures of slavery while listening to the song "Follow the Drinking Gourd" to lead them into a project about abolition.*

Sample Entry Document (Read aloud by a guest speaker, from the "Creatures of Oldham County" Spotlight Project)

Dear Kindergarten Students,

My name is Shauna and I work for the Oldham County Conservation District. We help people in our community by showing them how to take care of the land. I heard that the kindergarten students at St. Francis School were great scientists who might be able to help me with something I need for my job. I would like to have a picture book to teach the people who live in Oldham County about the life cycles of some animals that live here. You might have to do some research and work together to find information for your book. You will also have to become authors and illustrators. It may be hard work, but I know you can do it. Do you think you could help me?

Sincerely,
Shauna B.
District Program Coordinator

Mapping Out Daily Teaching and Learning Tasks

At this point you have envisioned the end of your project (how students will demonstrate what they've learned in the major products and presentations), and you have planned the beginning (the Entry Event). Now it's time to plan what goes in between. As you can tell by now, planning a project is different from planning a sequence of typical classroom activities. Activities can be planned on a daily basis, even the night before you teach. Don't try that with a project, because it all has to hang together. Each lesson or scaffolding the teacher provides and each task students do must fit into the organizing structure the project provides. To get where you want to go — high-quality products and presentations — the steps in the journey need to be mapped out.

Planning the day-to-day use of time is one of the trickiest parts of PBL. The days between the Entry Event and the final reflections are a mix of independent student work time, teacher-guided activities and, at times, good old-fashioned direct instruction — all wrapped up in the context of the project.

Plan Backwards from Major Products and the Presentation

A good way to plan your project's daily teaching and learning tasks is to make a list of the knowledge and skills students will need in order to create high-quality products and make the presentations that culminate the project. Then plan backwards from the end, by thinking about the learning experiences you will need to provide to build background knowledge for inquiry, scaffold the inquiry process, and give students the information and tools they will need to complete their work.

For example, imagine your project's major product is a museum exhibit about a historical event, time or place, as in our Spotlight Project "Parkland on Display." Think about what students will need to know and be able to do in order to create it and present it to visitors. Your list might look like this:

- What people, places, and events were important

- When and where key events took place

- What a museum exhibit looks like

- How to design an effective exhibit

- The purpose of a museum exhibit

- How to select representative and interesting images and artifacts

- How to write captions and other short informational text

- How to use oral communication skills

Then decide how students will learn each item on your list of what they need to know and be able to do. For example, to learn about the history of the community, the children took a field trip, heard from guest speakers, read primary and secondary source texts, and participated in lessons conducted by their teachers. To learn about creating museum exhibits, students visited websites of various museums co-created a rubric for an exhibit, and were provided with direct instruction in graphic design by the art teacher.

We've provided on page 129 a simple form called a "Project Teaching and Learning Guide" to help you plan backwards. See the completed example in *Useful Stuff*, page 149 from the "Creatures in Oldham County" Spotlight Project. Writing the Teaching and Learning Guide before creating the Project Calendar helps you make sure everything is aligned, and that you're not missing something important that students will need in order to create the major products and be ready for presentations. After you complete this step, use the Project Calendar to note exactly when the teaching and learning tasks will occur.

✳ USE THIS   PROJECT DESIGN: STUDENT LEARNING GUIDE (*page 129*)

Creating a Project Calendar

In the previous chapter you might have reviewed your school's annual calendar and your curriculum maps and picked an appropriate window of time during which your project can run. Now, as you're planning the details of your project, use your Teaching and Learning Guide to create a calendar showing what will happen each day. (You can cut and paste items from the Teaching and Learning Guide directly onto your Project Calendar if using the electronic version.)

After the project is launched you may want to share the calendar, or a simplified version of it, with parents. Upper elementary students should get a copy as well. Show it regularly to younger students, to remind them of project checkpoints and progress.

A Project Calendar is pretty simple — you can use your own, or use the blank one you may have copied from the back of this book. We have also provided an example of a completed Project Calendar from one of our Spotlight Projects.

Using the Workshop Model in PBL

Many elementary teachers are familiar with the Reader's and Writer's workshop format, and Math workshops are becoming more popular. The general format for a workshop can be applied to any subject area in a project. The workshop model is a lesson planning framework that is compatible with inquiry-based curriculum design models like PBL because workshops create the conditions for investigating, questioning, communicating, and collaboratively constructing knowledge.

Workshops may be used every day or once a week, depending on need. Workshop plans may vary in format, but typically contain the following components, which may vary in length:

- **Mini-Lesson** with clearly stated goals, focused on a specific skill, in which the teacher models the skill to be learned or the work to be produced (e.g., how to do research notes or how to create a project product)

- **Application** in which students have time to practice and apply what was modeled by the teacher

- **Critique and revision** protocols in which students share their work and the teacher does formative assessment

- **Debrief session** to discuss the work done and what was learned, which is often recorded on an "anchor chart" that serves as a reference

For more information, see Samantha Bennett's *That Workshop Book*, an excellent resource for teachers interested in learning more about how to use the workshop approach across the curriculum.

PROJECT CALENDAR FORM (*page 130-131*)
EXAMPLE COMPLETED PROJECT CALENDAR
(*page 150-151*)

Record the following on your calendar:

- The Entry Event that launches the project

- Daily teaching and learning tasks

- Checkpoints for completion of project steps

- Practice presentations

- Presentation schedule

- Target dates for completion of major products

- Tests or other summative assessments, if applicable for your grade level

- Time for reflection and celebration at the end of the project

For an example of how a teacher conducted daily lessons and project work time over a 3½ week period, see the *Managing PBL: A Portrait* on pages 75 to 84.

TIPS FROM THE **CLASSROOM**

Plan for Effective Work With Experts

One of the most valuable experiences children can have in PBL is to work with adult professionals, either in the field or in the classroom. These experts can provide information about a topic, teach skills, and help students with project tasks and products. Experts can work with students in person, or you can reach them online using email, Skype, or other tools. Here's how to make the process effective:

- Before students see an expert, discuss how to ask good questions and how to take notes

- Have students generate their own questions to ask an expert

- Be sure the expert can relate to children and speak at a level they can understand (coach him or her if needed)

- Have experts show examples of products and describe things they do on a day-to-day basis, to give students a concrete idea of their work

- Ask experts to share information about the standards used to critique products they create

- Ask experts to give preliminary feedback about student work in progress

- Invite experts to be part of the audience for presentations

Communicating With Parents

It's important not to miss this detail when planning your project: how you will let parents know what's going on, because PBL may be unfamiliar territory for them. Since most of them experienced traditional schooling, they know about and expect things like worksheets, memorizing for tests, book reports, and maybe making things like dioramas and posters. But if their son or daughter comes home talking about "my team" or a "Driving Question" or "the presentation," parents may have some questions. They also might need to help their child do some project work at home — so communicate with them early, often, and clearly.

Before you launch your project, send a letter home, post messages on your class or school website, talk to them when they visit school, send email, or do all of the above. If your school is using PBL as a school-wide practice, parents have probably already been informed about the what and why of it. If so, a brief reminder about the value of PBL is all you need to include in your communication about a particular project. However, if you know that most parents do not know about PBL and this is the first project their child will have encountered, give them a longer explanation of what PBL is and why you are using this teaching method, emphasizing the skills their child will build as result of PBL.

TEMPLATE FOR LETTER TO PARENTS (*page 137*)   ✱ USE THIS

To inform parents about the project:

- Give an overview of the project: the main idea, the Driving Question, the major products. Tell them what students will learn, in terms of content, skills, and other goals.

- Describe the process by which students will complete the project, including working in teams, doing research, perhaps going off campus or working with other adults or outside organizations.

- Explain how they can help their child with project work (making sure to explain what "inquiry" is and how there is no single "right answer" to the Driving Question — although there still could be wrong or inadequate answers).

- Provide the rubric for major products.

- Let them know the general time frame for the project, including when and where exhibitions and presentations will take place, if you would like them to attend.

- Update them on the children's progress during the project, and after it's over report on how successful it was (assuming it went well, of course!).

Forming Student Teams

Before launching your project, decide how you will organize students into teams for project work. This decision depends on the nature of your project, the products students need to create, and of course the culture of your classroom and your knowledge of your students.

To Team or Not to Team?

If you teach primary students, it often makes sense for the whole class to do a project together. (This can be true even in high school projects). The children might work in teams only for short, specific tasks rather than for the duration of the project.

Who places students in teams?

You as the teacher should decide who is on which team. This reflects the real world, where employees do not typically get to choose their team members for projects. People in leadership positions make these decisions! They assemble teams based on their knowledge of the individuals' areas of strength and their feelings about who will work best together with an ultimate goal of creating productive, cohesive work groups. You may give students an opportunity for some input in choosing their own teams, but remind them that the goal of a team is to complete a project well, not to have fun with your friends. Remind them also that the teacher always retains the power to change someone to another team.

What is the ideal number of team members?

PBL teachers report that *four* is the ideal number for team work. When the size increases, it is more difficult to ensure that all members of the team contribute their share of the work and have a strong voice in team discussions. Teams of three work well, too, although the workload might be heavy and that old social dynamic, "two's company, three's a crowd" might come into play. Some projects are done in pairs, but students don't learn as much about collaboration as they do in larger teams — and watch out for Presentation Day, when you find yourself with 14 presentations to sit through!

How do you decide who should be on a team?

Most teachers have some experience with placing students on teams, so we will not claim there is one absolute right way to do it. Teachers need to think carefully about who will work and learn well with other students and then try it out. If you make a mistake or things don't work out, team members can always be changed — even during the project if needed, or certainly for the next project. There is no perfect procedure for forming teams. However, we can offer a few tips gathered from PBL teachers:

- Heterogeneous teams are ideal. Consider the tasks required and include a mix of talents, since PBL draws on many skills.

- Strategically group students who are most likely to be supportive of one another, and not dominating.

- If students are English Learners, they may need someone else on the team who speaks their language, or at least teammates who are good communicators and find ways to include them.

- For some projects in which teams address different aspects of a topic or Driving Question, group students based on interest. For example, in the "Meet Our Animal Neighbors" project in *Managing PBL: A Portrait*, the teacher asked students to rank their preferences for which animals to study, then formed teams.

TIPS FROM THE **CLASSROOM**

Survey Students on Their Strengths

To help you assign students to teams with a mix of skills and talents, give them a survey or checklist.

Ask them to tell you what strengths they can bring to a team, such as:

- artist
- writer
- leader
- good at making or building things
- computer skills
- researcher
- reader
- good follower of directions
- organized

Finding and Arranging Resources

Running a project does not have to be a resource-intensive process, but it may be. Your project might require material resources such as books, art supplies, chart paper and whatever is needed for making products, and equipment such as LCD projectors, video cameras, and laptops. You may need human resources, including people from the community, other teachers, or experts reached online.

Let's look at our Spotlight Projects for some examples. In "Selling a Cell" Gina needed computers with Internet access, graph paper, and PowerPoint software—and guest speakers from cell phone service providers, and parents or guardians to be interviewed and hear the fifth graders' presentations about cell phone plans. In "Cool With School Rules" Dana and her first graders needed computers with Internet access, video cameras and monitors, poster paper, plus the school principal and a police officer. For "The Shrimp Project" the resource list grew to be extensive over the months as Laurette and her fourth graders contacted experts from several organizations, gathered planting supplies and tools for field work, created products using paper, computers, video cameras, and t-shirts, and made presentations in various locations.

You'll see a place to list the resources you need on the *Project Overview* form in *Useful Stuff*. We have one simple but important suggestion on this topic:

☑ *Arrange everything well in advance.*

Human Resources to Consider

- Older students, including middle and high school

- Parents with special expertise, interests, hobbies, or skills that connect to your project

- Other teachers, administrators, or staff members with special expertise

- School or district specialists in art, music, drama, technology, physical education

- Experts from local (or distant, reached online) nonprofit organizations

- People from local businesses and industry

- Local government officials and agency representatives, police and fire departments

- Technical school, college and university faculty

Material Resources as "Text Sets"

Text sets are collections of resources that connect to your project topic, collected in a box, tub or other container. They are designed to grab students' interest, generate questions, and build background knowledge about the topic. A text set can include a variety of items, because the term "text" is used broadly. It can include fiction and non-fiction books, maps, informational pamphlets, poetry, Web documents, and entries from children's encyclopedias. See the *Bulletin Board* on page 72 for a list of online sources of materials.

Written material should vary by reading difficulty and the contents should appeal to a wide range of interests related to the project topic. But "text" could also be compelling images, artwork, or even an object. Allowing students to touch, investigate and wonder about objects connected to the project topic is a great way to spark curiosity. If your students are studying geology, for example, gather different types of small rocks and place them in zip-lock bags or clear containers and insert text descriptions for each object.

Text sets can be used in a variety of ways throughout a project:

- Early on in the project, allow student teams to informally browse through the text set to arouse their curiosity about the topic and record initial questions for further inquiry.

- Place text sets at student tables for silent reading.

- Allow students to browse through the materials after finishing independent work.

- Assist students in finding a "just right text" from the set to use during the application phase in a Reader's Workshop.

Search PowerPoints for Material for Beginning Readers

It can be difficult to find materials, especially non-fiction, appropriate for emergent or beginning readers. Try the following search on your Web browser:

"(project-related word) + PowerPoint"

For example:

"Habitat + PowerPoint"
or
"Polar Bear + PowerPoint"

You will likely find a number of interesting PowerPoint slides related to your topic that contain a combination of text and compelling images. If the level is too difficult for your readers, do some editing to make the text more appropriate. When printed out, these PowerPoints can serve as non-fiction "books" for your students. Save the original non-edited version of the PowerPoint for your advanced readers. This way, you'll have two non-fiction "books" on the same topic with varied reading levels.

 **Bulletin Board** Online Sources of Text Set Materials

You can create a "digital text set" by finding materials on the Internet to post on a shared workspace like a Wiki. Older elementary students can be given access to these materials, or for younger students, print them for inclusion in text set containers in the classroom. Here are some websites that teachers recommend:

Non-fiction reading:
- **biguniverse.com** — Big Universe Learning (fee-based) online reading & writing community
- **en.childrenslibrary.org** — International Children's Digital Library

Non-fiction printable PowerPoints:
- **tes.co.uk/teaching-resources** — TES Connect has many resources for educators, under the auspices of TSL Education Ltd., a leading educational publisher in the U.K.

Maps:
- **nationalgeographic.com/xpeditions/atlas** — National Geographic Xpeditions Atlas
- **infoplease.com/atlas** — InfoPlease has maps, country profiles, statistics

Poetry:
- **poetryfoundation.org** — Poetry Foundation's searchable archive, news, articles
- **poets.org** — Academy of American Poets archive sorted by poet, poem, topic

Images:
- **nationalgeographicstock.com** — National Geographic stock photos
- **worldimages.sjsu.edu** — WorldImages database by CA State University
- **corbisimages.com** — Corbis Images archive (free to print with watermark)
- **timelifepictures.com** — Time & Life Magazines' photographs of American history

Primary source documents and diaries:
- **gilderlehrman.org** — Gilder Lehrman Institute of American History
- **memory.loc.gov** — Library of Congress American Memory Project
- **chroniclingamerica.loc.gov** — Library of Congress American newspaper archive

Artwork:
- **artcyclopedia.com** — Artcyclopedia is an extensive, searchable database
- **abcgallery.com** — Olga's Gallery has a large, searchable collection

Entries from children's encyclopedias:
- **kids.britannica.com** — Encyclopedia Britannica Kids (fee-based)

Before Moving on to the Next Chapter

If you've been using the *Project Overview* form to record your project plans as you moved through this chapter, you should have filled in this much so far:

PROJECT DESIGN: OVERVIEW

page 1

Name of Project:	**Duration:**
Subject/Course:	**Teacher(s):**	**Grade Level:**

Other subject areas to be included, if any:

Key Knowledge and Understanding (CCSS or other standards)	
Success Skills (to be taught and assessed)	Critical Thinking/Problem Solving	Management
	Collaboration	Other:
Project Summary (include student role, issue, problem or challenge, action taken, and purpose/beneficiary)	
Driving Question	
Entry Event	
Products	Individual:	Specific content and competencies to be assessed:
	Team:	Specific content and competencies to be assessed:

DONE

PROJECT DESIGN: OVERVIEW

page 2

Making Products Public (include how the products will be made public and who students will engage with during/ at end of project)	
Resources Needed	On-site people, facilities:
	Equipment:
	Materials:
	Community Resources:

Reflection Methods (how individual, team, and/or whole class will reflect during/at end of project)	Journal/Learning Log		Focus Group	
	Whole-Class Discussion		Fishbowl Discussion	
	Survey		Other:	

Notes:

DONE

In *Useful Stuff* on page 147-148 you can find a completed Project Overview form, from our "Pizza and the World of Work" Spotlight Project.

Ready, set, go — it's time to discuss how to manage your project. If you'd like to get a detailed, day-to-day picture of how a teacher manages a project, read the following special section, *Managing PBL: A Portrait*. The next chapter, *Managing Your Project*, contains our guidance, tools, and tips.

TIPS FROM THE **CLASSROOM**

Don't Carve Your Plan in Stone

Don't get too attached to every detail in your project plan — stay flexible. The path your project takes may change to some extent, because PBL is never fully predictable. You might see the need to make adjustments, and your students might have a voice in some decisions and make independent choices that will affect the journey. Also, students may need information or ask for help in ways you did not anticipate, delaying the project.

Managing PBL:
A PORTRAIT

Before we get to the next chapter, *Managing Your Project*, let's pause to see what a project looks like as it unfolds in a classroom. The following story is fictitious. We chose to make this a 2nd grade project, because that grade level shares some characteristics of first grade and kindergarten, yet upper elementary teachers will also see applications for their classrooms. The school where this might take place uses a partially integrated PBL model, where most project work occurs in the afternoon in science and social studies focused projects, but some of the work is incorporated into the morning literacy block in read-alouds, guided reading, and writing instruction.

Meet Our Animal Neighbors

Project: Meet Our Animal Neighbors

Setting: Anywhere, USA

Details: 2nd grade; Science and Language Arts; 3½ weeks

Idea & Product: Create text and illustrations for the school website about wild animals that live near the school

Content standards to be learned:

- Compare and contrast groups of animals (e.g., insects, birds, fish, mammals) and look at how animals in these groups are more similar to one another than to animals in other groups.

- Identify the ways in which an organism's habitat provides for its basic needs.

- Investigate and understand that behavioral and physical adaptations help animals survive.

Driving Question: How can we make pages for our school website that tell people about the animals that live near our school?

Project Launch (Days 1-2)

The teacher's goals for the first two days are to introduce the project, generate student interest and questions, and begin building knowledge about the topic.

The teacher launched the project after lunch on a Monday in April. He began by asking his second graders a question: "How many different wild animals do you think live near our school?" After some discussion of what "wild" meant and how far "near" extended, students began naming animals. Their answers ranged from birds and rodents to spiders and insects — after clarifying that the latter two were indeed "animals," drawing from what students had learned in first grade. The teacher said, "Let's find out! We're going on a walk around the neighborhood.

> *From the Desk of:*
> *Principal Skinner*
>
> Dear Students,
>
> I am asking you to help us put something new on our school's website! We would like to tell people about the community around our school. One of the things I thought people might want to know is, "What animals live near our school?" I would like your class to make new pages for our website, using words and pictures to tell about the animals.
>
> As you might remember, we have a sister school that is in a very different kind of place. Their second graders are going to make the same thing for their website. They will be looking at your web pages, so it's important to do a good job! Please show me your web pages in three weeks. Thank you very much.
>
> Sincerely,
> Mr. Skinner

I'd like you to look around and try to see as many different animals as you can..." He and the children talked about how they might see evidence of animals such as nests, spider webs, gopher holes, feathers and droppings, and so on. He gave them all clipboards with T-charts headed "animals/evidence" and modeled how

to use it by showing an example on a document camera. During the walk the class stopped at the nearby park to record what they had observed in words and drawings. The teacher circulated from student to student and reviewed their notes, asked probing questions, and made suggestions.

The next afternoon, the teacher displayed a letter from the principal and read it aloud (see letter on page 76).

Although they had seen it before, the teacher showed the children the school's website using the Smart Board. He pointed out the section titled "Our Community," which had only a brief written description and a photo of the school seen from across the street. Back on the home page, he clicked on the link to their sister school and opened up its website, which had a similar section about its very different community. Then he paused and picked up a rolled-up piece of chart paper, which he taped to the wall in the front of the room, revealing the Driving Question:

How can we make pages for our school website that tell people about the animals that live near our school?

He said, "This is the question we're going be answering in this project" and read it aloud. Encouraging students to ask questions about the project, he got them excited by telling them they were going to be doing more field work, use the Internet, and work with the tech teacher to take pictures with digital cameras and upload them to their web pages.

After distributing the clipboards from the neighborhood walk experience, the teacher facilitated a "Think-Pair-Share" discussion. Students looked over their notes and drawings, then paired up to talk with a partner about something they had observed on the walk and tried to come up with a lingering question. They shared observations and questions as whole class, as the teacher led them in co-constructing a "Know/Want to Know/Learned" (KWL) chart. They listed what they knew about local animals, what they wanted to learn about them, and left the third column blank so they could record what

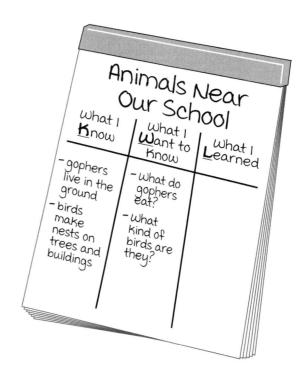

they were learning during the project. One girl started the discussion by saying she saw a bird's nest up in a tree. The teacher asked her what she "knows" about birds' nests, and she said, "some birds make nests in trees but some make them in buildings. She "wanted to know" what kind of bird made the nest in the tree. In addition to what they had observed, some students insisted they should include animals that were "hiding" in buildings or in the ground, such as insects and spiders, so the list was expanded beyond what they had observed. And some students knew there were frogs, salamanders, turtles, and snakes not too far away, so they made the list too. The teacher wrote the name of each animal the class was considering for the web page on a strip of paper, and placed it in a pocket chart.

Building General Knowledge (Days 3-6)

Over the next several days the teacher continues to build students' general knowledge about animals, combined with activities that reinforce literacy skills.

On the third day, the teacher gave each student a research notebook—a folder with several sheets of paper inside divided into two columns headed "What I Want to Know" and "What I Learned." He modeled how to use it to record their questions about animals on the left side, and write notes, make drawings, or add pictures about what they learn on the right side.

During "project work time" in the afternoon, the teacher placed a project "text set" at each table. The text set included general information about animal habitats and adaptations, along with a variety of items related to local

animals. The items included bags of objects (such as feathers, a bird's egg, a pine cone chewed by a squirrel) with written descriptions of them, fiction and non-fiction books, a map of the neighborhood, poetry, photos, drawings, and excerpts from articles, websites and encyclopedias geared toward young children. After showing a few examples of what was in it to spark the students' curiosity, he encouraged them to select items from the text set during silent reading time. As they examined the text set, the students recorded questions and answers if they found them on the "What I Want to Know" and "What I Learned" pages in their research notebooks.

During Reader's Workshop in the morning, the teacher incorporated read-aloud books and guided reading books that helped students gain more knowledge about the project topic. The books were aligned with the knowledge and concepts about animal characteristics and their habitats stated in the 2nd grade science

standards. Gradually, he began to incorporate more specific texts about insects, birds, spiders, and small mammals like those that lived near the school.

The class began to co-construct a "concept wall" about animals, coached by the teacher. He posted three headings for columns on the wall: "Animal, Adaptation, Advantage." (They later wrote, for example, "Animal — gray squirrel; Adaptation — big front teeth; Advantage — chew hard food.") Underneath each heading, the children began to post words and pictures related to it.

The teacher conducted short science lessons to build students' knowledge of topics from the standards. He tied the lessons to the questions students put on the KWL chart. For example, to teach the class about different types of adaptations to habitat, he used the ground squirrel as an example. They learned how the animal transports food in cheek pouches (a structure), communicates the presence of danger with its voice (a behavior) and hibernates to survive the winter (physiology). Each afternoon in a whole-class discussion, the class kept track of what they were learning by referring and adding to the KWL chart.

In preparation for the next phase of the project in which the students would engage in an in-depth investigation of an animal, the teacher sent a letter to parents. The letter explained the project, invited parents to attend presentations, and asked for their help with some homework. He asked them to find out from their son or daughter what particular animal they were studying, and help them make observations of it when they could. For example, if they were in the back yard or at the park, look for gopher holes or try to spot birds, and record notes in their research notebook. He also posted the letter on his class website and updated parents during the project.

Organizing Teams and Tasks
(Day 6-7)

By the end of the first week of the project, the teacher sees that the children are ready to begin narrowing their focus. Through observation and other checks for understanding, he knows the students have enough general knowledge about the topic to allow them to do further in-depth inquiry about one particular animal for the website. His goal for the second week is to form teams, establish norms for collaboration, and get them started on their research.

The teacher had planned to form six groups composed of four students. He reviewed the list of animals generated by the students that he had displayed in the pocket chart, and sorted them into categories: insects, birds, arachnids, reptiles, amphibians, and mammals. He made labels to insert as headers on the chart. He decided that reptiles and amphibians would be combined into one group because there were only a couple of types of each in their area. Near the end of project work time on Monday of the second week, he displayed the pocket chart listing the five groups of animals and told the children they would be working on a team that was going to study one type of animal to make a web page about. He gave each student a "ballot" and had them rank their choices, telling them he would announce the teams on Tuesday. Since

Ballot
5 insects
1 birds
6 arachnids
3 reptiles
4 amphibians
2 mammals

a lot of students chose birds, and there were a lot of different birds in their area, he made two bird teams. He balanced the teams to make sure everyone who might need a little extra support from teammates was taken care of.

On Tuesday he announced the teams, seated them at their tables, and explained how important it would be for everyone to work well together. He explained that teams would have to make important decisions about what to include on their page of the website. They needed to decide which animals to feature on their page and who would be responsible for each part. He told them this requires strong teamwork, because they have to listen to each member's ideas and decide as a group. He facilitated a class discussion on the topic, "What does it look like and sound like when a team is working well together?" and listed the students' ideas on the board. They gave examples of norms such as, "everyone listens when someone talks" and "everyone does what they're supposed to do" and "nobody is messing around."

The teacher displayed on the Smart Board a rubric for collaboration skills, read it over with the class, and asked them if they would add anything to it based on their discussion. After making a few changes and additions, he said, "Let's practice using this with an example." He had planned a fishbowl discussion to model collaboration skills, using the development of a team contract as the team's task. He identified one representative from each team to participate

in the fishbowl at a table in the center of the room and had the remaining students form a circle of observers around the fishbowl. He asked the observers to use the rubric to look for evidence that the fishbowl team was working well together during the activity.

He reviewed the directions for the activity. The fishbowl team was asked to model the process of filling out a contract to govern their team work. One child was appointed to serve as the facilitator and another was asked to serve as the recorder. The teacher reminded them about each role by pointing to the list of duties on the wall, which were used for all small-group activities during the year. He especially noted that the facilitator was to "help the group stay focused" rather than "be a bossy leader." The fishbowl team followed these steps:

1. Review the list of norms from the class discussion

2. Discuss whether they should add any additional norms

3. Decide on one or two additional norms if they wish

4. Write all the norms as "We promise to…" statements on the contract

5. Sign their names on the contract

The teacher then facilitated a debrief discussion in which the observers offered comments about the teamwork skills they observed and asked clarifying questions about the task.

The teams returned to their tables and the teacher distributed templates for team contracts, for students to fill in. Each team also received one blue-colored "Recorder" card and one red-colored "Facilitator" card. The teacher asked the teams to identify a recorder and a facilitator, who placed their cards in front of them to indicate the group's decision. Each team then replicated the process modeled by the fishbowl team, agreeing on norms and filling out and signing the contract. If one team finished before others, the teacher instructed students to select an item from the project text set to read quietly. He circulated around the room, conferred with groups and reviewed contracts, and signed each one.

Throughout the remainder of the project, the teacher continued to use strategies to build cohesion and independence within each team. Their first task, for example, was to come up with a team motto that related somehow to their type of animal. He facilitated regular fishbowl sessions, incorporated a few team building activities, and had ongoing dialog with individual teams and the class as a whole regarding their progress in meeting their established norms. One of the class's favorite team-building activities, designed to promote effective communication within teams, was

a story builder activity in which the teacher distributed cut-apart comic strips and had students draw sections at random and work as a team to put the comic strip back in order. After each of these activities, the class discussed the role played by teamwork, communication, and critical thinking and problem solving skills.

Focused Inquiry and Specific Content Knowledge (Days 7-11)

Now that student teams are formed and ready for work, the teacher guides them in generating and finding answers to questions about their specific type of animal. He provides tools to assist them in the research process, and conducts reading activities and lessons about specific science topics aligned to the relevant standards.

Now it was time to focus the students on two things: which specific animals they were going to put on the website, and what they would need to learn about them. At this point in the process the teacher wanted to establish a timeline for completion of the project, so he showed students a project calendar on the Smart Board. Important checkpoints were noted for written drafts of text, illustrations and web page plans, and also practice presentations and the day of their presentations. He brought this calendar up daily to remind students where they were in the project.

The teacher showed a list of animals they had observed on their neighborhood walk, and pointed out that he had put them in categories and added the exact name of a few animals they were not able to identify precisely. Each student team met for 10 minutes to decide which particular animals they were going to include on their web page. (One birds team, for example, chose blue jays, crows, starlings, and hummingbirds. The other birds team had a different list to choose from.) They filled out a

"Task List" to record which team member would study which animal in depth and write the text and prepare illustrations about it for the website. The teacher walked around the room to monitor the students' collaboration skills and decision-making process, coaching them when necessary.

The teacher showed students the list they made after the neighborhood walk, including what a visitor to their web page might want to know about the animals. He asked the children to take 10 minutes to discuss in their teams what else they wanted to include on the list. Because they had gained more knowledge about the topic during the past week, the students had a lot of ideas. The teacher facilitated a whole-class discussion to reach agreement and make a list of what information should be provided about each animal. He was careful to check that the information they were including was focused on topics defined by the standards for 2nd grade biological science.

For example, the students suggested "what the animals look like," "how big they are" and "where they live," which corresponded to the standards' references to comparing and contrasting groups of animals, habitats and adaptations. If something was being missed, the teacher asked questions that led the students toward the standards. For example, when no one suggested anything about how a habitat changes with the seasons, he asked, "What about the winter? Doesn't that change the animal's habitat?" This

caused the students to ask questions about adaptations such as hibernation, longer fur, migration, and so on. The class agreed on the following list of information about each animal to put on the web pages:

- name of animal

- what it looks like (color, size, fur, feathers, skin, etc.)

- what it eats

- where it lives (habitat) during different times of the year

- how its habitat affects what it looks like and how it behaves

- some interesting things about it (our choice)

Over the next several days, the teacher facilitated more science lessons, aligned with the information students would need to know to create their web page. The students also brought animal observation notes from home during this time. The class took another walk around their neighborhood, this time with specific questions in their research notebooks to guide them as they observed their animal's habitat and, occasionally, an individual animal or signs of it. The tech teacher accompanied them and helped them use a digital camera to take photographs.

The teacher also allowed time for students to begin writing drafts of text for their web page, and assemble or create pictures to go with it. At checkpoints he had students give each other peer feedback on their work, along with his own. Each team also used the collaboration rubric and their contract to reflect on how well they were working together, as the teacher met with each team to hear their thoughts and offer feedback and coaching. Occasionally during this and all phases of the project, the teacher also pointed out when the students were being good critical thinkers and problem solvers, and coached them in the use of these skills through modeling with a "think aloud" process.

Literacy was incorporated into project work by using a literature circle format to read and discuss texts related to their topic. At first, the teacher selected the text related to animals in the assigned category for each team. Later he allowed teams to request materials about their animals by using a simple "text request" form, on which they could indicate what specific information they wanted. He used the forms to assess how well each team was progressing, steering them toward particular material if it looked like they needed it.

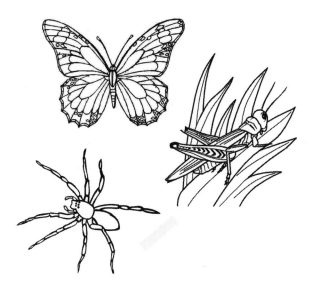

Creating Products (Days 11-14)

After the students gain enough knowledge about their particular animals, and record notes in their research notebooks that answer key questions, the teacher focuses the teams on the task of creating their web page.

On the first day of the third week, the teacher took the children to the computer room, where the technology teacher showed them how they were going to create web pages with text and pictures. The teachers displayed a few examples of web pages from various State Parks describing native animals, and then led the students in brainstorming and recording some ideas about how their pages might be organized. The class created a list headed, "What a good web page is like" by naming characteristics such as "easy to read," "has different parts," "correct and interesting information and pictures," "captions for pictures," and "colorful," and "not too crowded." The technology teacher showed students a rubric for a good web page, which the class discussed and modified if necessary, based on their discussion. Each team was given a set of guidelines which described in student-friendly language the steps for creating a web page.

Back in their classroom, the teacher guided students to create the final text for their web pages using a series of writer's workshops, providing time for modeling, application, feedback, and revision. With help from the tech teacher, the teams assembled their text and illustrations on their web pages, checking themselves with the rubric until they were satisfied with their work.

Presentation and Reflection
(Days 15-18)

Finally, the teams are ready to practice their presentations and show their web pages to the principal, parents, and sister school. After this culminating event, the teacher leads students in reflecting on what they learned and how they worked during the project.

Now that the students' web pages were complete, they were ready to show their work. The teacher had arranged for the principal to visit their classroom, and invited parents too. But first, the children had to practice, although they had been taught some public speaking skills earlier in the year. The teacher modeled a flawed one-minute presentation in a humorous way, and asked the students to give him feedback based on the rubric. Then he made another, much improved presentation, which the students scored much higher on the rubric.

The teacher distributed a "Presentation Planning Form," showed the teams how to use it, and gave them time to work. He went from team to team, coaching them to organize their presentations and polish up their delivery. The teams made practice presentations to each other and the class, gave each other feedback and made adjustments, a process that continued into the following day. Excitement — and a little nervousness — was building.

On presentation day the principal arrived in class, along with the tech teacher and some parents. Each team presented its web page and answered questions. The teacher, audience and the other teams scored each presentation with the rubric. After getting the thumbs-up from the principal, the students went to the computer room to upload their web pages to their school's website.

The next day they looked at what the students at their sister school had put on its website and discussed the similarities and differences between the animals in their areas. (Next time, the teacher noted, he would have students connect with their sister school during the project at checkpoints to compare notes.) The teacher used this occasion to firm up the students' understanding of key science concepts and vocabulary.

Each team met one last time to go over the collaboration rubric and give themselves a summative evaluation, writing a short note to the teacher reflecting on strengths and areas for improvement. The teacher facilitated a discussion in which the class reflected on the overall success of the project, including what went well and areas that could be improved. Finally, based on an earlier request from the children, the class returned to the park, where they ate lunch and celebrated their accomplishments.

MANAGING YOUR PROJECT

This Chapter's Goal

All set? You've got your project idea, you've planned and prepared, and now it's ready for launch. In this chapter we'll discuss how to effectively manage the implementation of your project, including:

- Creating a Culture of Inquiry in Your Classroom

- Beginning the Inquiry Process after the Entry Event

- Building Collaboration Skills and Managing Student Teams

- Teaching Students How to Think Critically

- Using Formative Assessment and Setting Checkpoints

- Preparing for and Facilitating Presentations to an Audience

Creating a Culture of Inquiry in Your Classroom

As we've said, one of the most important features of PBL is *inquiry*. By that we mean more than giving students a list of questions to answer by checking reference books or websites. Inquiry in PBL means students *ask* their own questions, use a variety of sources to develop not-always-obvious answers, reflect on what they find, then ask deeper questions—always guided by the Driving Question of the project.

As you design and manage your project, ask yourself these questions to check if you're providing students with opportunities for inquiry and creating a culture that supports it:

- *Am I allowing students generate their own research questions?*

   After launching the project by sharing the Driving Question with the students, have them brainstorm other questions that relate to it. As the project unfolds and students build background knowledge about the topic, they can sharpen this list with their own questions — ones they care about. Students often develop passionate interests in PBL, so let them explore.

- *Am I letting students know the project is truly open-ended?*

   Some teachers, in attempting to facilitate inquiry, lead students down predetermined paths because the process seems more manageable to facilitate when it is tightly controlled. Students can sense when they are being directed as opposed to being given ownership of the process. Through your words and actions, make it clear the project is flexible enough to allow creative, innovative ideas to emerge. If students want to take the project in a certain direction and are posing questions you didn't anticipate, let them do so as long as important standards are still the focus.

- *Am I coaching students to use many methods of investigation and sources of information?*

   Design your project so students investigate using such tools as interview, observation, survey, viewing, experimenting, and critical reading. Coach students to synthesize what they learn from various sources, to encourage creativity and critical thinking.

- *Am I giving students the chance to wonder, research, and share as a learning community?*

   Inquiry is better when students can talk with peers and as a whole class, with the teacher as facilitator. Students broaden and deepen their thinking when they discuss what questions to investigate, compare notes and

Set Up Your Space for PBL

To set up your classroom space to support project work, visualize your project in progress. Imagine your students engaged in teamwork, doing research, sharing supplies, participating in mini-lessons, creating products, making presentations, and so on.

PBL teachers make these recommendations:

- Have tables for student teams, or desks that can easily be arranged to form a shared workspace.

- Have computers available in the room (rather than somewhere across the campus).

- Carve out space (and get a rug) if you want teams of students to gather around you on the floor for mini-lessons or fishbowl modeling sessions.

- Keep supplies for project work in one location, organized and easily accessible

- Post important documents on the wall, such as the Driving Question, Need to Know or KWL lists, Project Calendar, Word/ Concept Wall, norms for team work, sample products with rubrics, etc.

- Have a small table where you can meet with team representatives.

Note: Some teachers involve students in planning the classroom layout—you could even have them submit design proposals!

---

conclusions, share experiences, and decide together what new questions should be asked. Collaborative inquiry builds excitement and engagement, too. Let students know that it's important to listen to others' ideas and contribute to the group's understanding.

- *Am I including opportunities for students to reflect on their learning throughout the project?*

Reflection should be an integral part of the inquiry process. Provide time during the project, not just at the end, for students to pause and look back on their questions, their research strategies, and their conclusions. Ask them to evaluate and make observations about what they did, and make new decisions if needed.

Beginning the Inquiry Process
after the Entry Event

After the Entry Event you need to start students on the path toward completion of the project. The basic goal of "phase two" of the project launch is to begin the inquiry process by generating student questions and ideas about the topic and their task. You'll also want to familiarize students with the goals and general plan for the project.

After an Entry Event, build on the momentum to begin the inquiry process with the following steps:

1. Share the Driving Question with students, or have them write it with you.

2. Tell students, in general terms, about the culminating products and presentations.

3. Conduct a discussion to generate questions and ideas the children are wondering about related to the topic, the Driving Question, and their task. If you think they are ready, focus students on what they think they will need to know in order to complete the project. (See below for details on how to conduct a structured "Need to Know" discussion.)

4. Explain the project's logistical details, either orally and/or on a handout. If you have planned to begin the project with team work, let students know who will be working with. If appropriate for your grade level, show students the Project Calendar with target dates, checkpoints, and major events.

How to Conduct a "Need to Know" Discussion

Creating a "need to know" list helps students get a clear idea of their task at the start of a project, guides them in inquiry, and should be used to check progress along the way. It is more appropriate for upper elementary students, since younger children may not be able to identify what they think they need to know. (See the *K-2 How-To* box on page 91 for tips on using the "KWL" format as an alternative.)

1. Review the major products and presentations students will need to complete for the project. Then, ask them to think about what they would need to know in order to successfully do the task.

   Tip: If you think students may need help getting started — or you are met with blank looks — have them generate some items for the list by talking with a partner or in small groups. You also could model the process with some examples, especially with younger students who may be new to this kind of thinking.

Questions from the Discussion of the Driving Question in "The Shrimp Project"

After the Entry Event—a video documentary about threatened animal species—and the introduction of the Driving Question, "What can we do to save endangered species?" Laurette's 4th graders came up with the following list of questions to start their inquiry, which were later sorted into categories:

- Who is working to save endangered species – can we raise money to send to them?

- How can we raise a lot of money? Can we make and sell something?

- Can we tell our parents and other people about how they can help?

- What species are closest to becoming extinct? Where do they live?

- Can the president or governor or other leaders do anything?

- What are ALL the reasons why species are endangered?

- Can we make a protest somewhere? Can we make signs?

- Are there any species near us that we can help save?

- When are we going to start and how long are we going to do this project?

- Can we watch more videos or read about other endangered species and how to save them?

Note: In most projects, unlike this one, the teacher has already decided what the major products will be, how they will be presented, how standards will be taught and assessed, and so on. Laurette had to plan this project "on the fly."

2. On a flipchart, the board, or a computer projector so everyone can see, write the words, "What Do We Need to Know?"

   Tip: *If appropriate for your grade level, ask for a volunteer to be a recorder. This frees you to facilitate the discussion.*

3. Record all ideas and questions on the appropriate chart/column, capturing students' own wording. They can suggest things they need to know about the content/topic *and* the process.

   Tip: *You may edit a bit for clarity, but do not try to reshape students' questions and comments or it will feel like you're making the words yours when they should be "owned" by students, in a PBL culture of inquiry and independence.*

Sample "Need to Know" Lists

From the *Cool With School Rules* Spotlight Project:	**From the *What's With This Guy?* Spotlight Project:**
The 1st graders in Dana's class asked the following questions after the request from their principal for help in creating rules for various places around the school:	The 5th graders in Aaron's class asked the following questions after meeting the patient with the mystery ailment. Some questions, they later realized, were not relevant:

From the *Cool With School Rules* Spotlight Project:

▶ How many rules should we make?

▶ How big should our posters be?

▶ Who's going to watch our video?

▶ Are the rules for just us or the whole school?

▶ What if the other kids don't follow the rules?

▶ Why do we have to make the rules?

From the *What's With This Guy?* Spotlight Project:

▶ How old is this patient?

▶ Has he been sick before?

▶ Why did his girlfriend have to make him come in?

▶ What diseases can cause these symptoms?

▶ What else might be wrong with him? Can we do a blood test? Get an x-ray?

▶ When do we have to present our decision?

▶ How long does our presentation have to be?

4. Do not attempt to answer questions yet.

   Tip: Resist the urge, although this may seem counterintuitive and certainly flies in the face of traditional teaching practice. Remember, in PBL you want to encourage students to find answers by working independently as much as possible.

5. Prompt students to add to the list if you notice they are not identifying "need to knows" that *you* know they will need, especially if it relates to key content knowledge which students may not gravitate toward.

   Tip: Do this subtly, like Socrates would have done. Ask, "How about this part of the project — what would you need to learn to be able to do that?" or "Do you have any questions about the part of our topic about _____?"

6. Keep the "need to know" list on display and revisit it frequently as a management tool during the project. Check items off the list as they become "known" and add new items as they emerge.

   Tip: When you introduce a lesson or provide a resource to students, point to the need to know list to remind students that they identified it as something that will help them with their project. This helps students see the context and feel like their voice has been heard. Ask them if they have new questions as they learn more — and deadlines approach.

Facilitating the Inquiry Process

After the project is launched, help your students find answers to the questions they think they need to know in order to address the Driving Question for the project. You can provide them with some answers through direct instruction, but coach them to investigate some questions using an inquiry process. Depending on the age and skill level of your students, you might need to coach them closely and provide substantial scaffolding to guide inquiry, or you might be able to give them quite a bit of independence.

K-2 How-to

K-W-L Charts vs. Need to Know Lists

In lower elementary classes, PBL teachers sometimes elect to use the popular "Know/ Want to Learn/ Learned" 3-column chart to document the inquiry process. It differs from a "need to know" list, where the questions are more focused on the specific task required by the project. A KWL starts by activating students' prior knowledge of a topic. The middle column lists questions about the project topic, not just about the task itself. The "Learned" column is for recording the knowledge students gain during the project. If you're more comfortable with a KWL chart and think it's more appropriate, use this strategy instead of the "Need to Know" list.

The type of support you provide will also need to align with your school's literacy model. We've provided a sample below of the steps you could take to facilitate inquiry in a project, which includes several literacy-building strategies. The basic process is to start by building students' knowledge of the project topic, then to coach them in asking further questions, then to guide them in using a variety of resources that help answer their questions and successfully complete project products.

If you teach younger students, provide them with more direct support. Help them find texts at the right level. Schedule lessons on how to be a researcher in which you model the process of searching for and recording answers to questions. Model how to read a text with a question in mind. If, to address students' questions, you can only find text that is too advanced, summarize the key points—or find videos on YouTube that are easier to understand. Confer regularly with students and groups to note their progress in recording and finding answers to questions. (If you haven't already seen it, the *Managing PBL: A Portrait* on page 75 provides a detailed look at how a 2nd grade teacher facilitates the inquiry process.)

Sample Steps for Facilitating Inquiry in a Project:

1. **Share books, articles, pictures, or other text** you've assembled for the project, for students to use to investigate the project topic and answer their "need to know" questions.

2. **Distribute note-taking guides or other materials to record information** during their investigation. (See the *Tip from the Classroom* on the next page on Research Notebooks.)

3. **Facilitate a Reader's Workshop series**, using fiction and/or non-fiction to build background knowledge for inquiry and generate deeper questions from students.

4. **Begin to create a word/concept wall** to record and display words related to the content knowledge and conceptual understanding needed for the project, for students to use as a reference when writing during the project.

5. **Conduct a series of lessons or workshops to teach specific content related to the topic**. (See description of how to use the workshop approach across the curriculum on page 65.)

6. **Launch literature circles with books related to the inquiry topic**. (See description of how to facilitate literature circles on page 54.)

7. **Provide additional experiences** such as field work, visits with experts, and the use of online resources to help answer students' questions and gain the knowledge they need.

Use Research Notebooks to Guide and Document Inquiry

Research notebooks are helpful for recording questions and organizing information related to the inquiry process in a project. Give one to each student. The contents could include:

- Questions students need or want to find answers to

- Answers to students' questions

- List of sources of information used

- Questions for expert visitors

- Data, sketches, and reflections from in-class investigations and field experiences

- Graphic organizers for information

- Reflections on the Driving Question

- Reflections on how their thinking has changed

Building Collaboration Skills and Managing Student Teams

Even if you carefully chose students for teams, it doesn't mean they will work together effectively. It's often hard enough for adults in the workplace to function well as a team. You need to build your students' collaboration skills and monitor them during the project, intervening if necessary. How much you do this depends on your students' level of experience. Perhaps you've already used cooperative learning strategies in your classroom or school, or students have had other experience with working in teams. If so, great—you won't need to scaffold their collaboration skills during your project as much as you will if they are new to the process.

There are two general ways to scaffold collaboration skills. One is to provide them with tools such as forms, templates, rubrics and other self-assessment guidelines. The other type of scaffolding is less formal; you coach students by modeling behaviors for them, talking with them as they work, and giving

Build collaboration skills *before* launching your project.

If your students are not used to working in teams, spend a little time preparing them for team work before your project starts. Use activities like these examples, followed by a discussion on the use of collaboration (and communication or even problem-solving skills):

- Start the year with team-building activities, such as games and get-to-know-you conversations, and revisit them before the start of a project.

- Do short, fun activities — like, say, building a tower with popsicle sticks — in which students learn how to take various roles, such as materials-getter, recorder, facilitator, and evaluator.

- Have teams complete a chart of the tasks they would assign to each member if they were doing a silly "project" such as "Plan a trip as if you were a group of monkeys going to the North Pole."

- Practice how to make a decision by consensus, using an engaging topic such as "What should we have for a snack after school?"

them feedback on how they're doing. The following steps contain guidance for both types of scaffolding.

Step One: Help students understand what good collaboration means.

Discuss with the whole class what it means to work effectively as a team. Ask students to describe what you would see and hear when this is happening. For example, students might say "we listen to each other," "we do our share of the work," and "we help and respect each other." Construct a list and keep it posted. (These are sometimes called "ground rules," "norms," or "expectations.") Or, instead of a list, write a collaboration rubric with your students.

If you don't want to write a rubric with students, show them one that has already been developed, like the collaboration rubrics we provide in *Useful Stuff*. Take time to help them read and understand it.

Another effective way to show students what good collaboration means is to model it with a "live" demonstration. Have observers use the rubric, which is the best way to show students what it means. See the *Bulletin Board* on page 96 for directions for a "fishbowl-style" modeling process.

✱ USE THIS **SAMPLE COLLABORATION RUBRICS** (*page 134, 136*)

Step Two: Provide students with tools: contracts and work planning forms.

In secondary PBL classrooms, where students have a greater degree of independence when doing project work in teams, teachers often have students use contracts to clearly spell out details such as the roles of various team members, how they expect work to be done, and procedures for handling situations in which team members do not follow through on assigned tasks. Although an elementary school teacher would monitor teams more closely and intervene if problems are occurring, a contract is still a good idea. This formality creates a level of seriousness about working together and gives young students a snapshot of what it is like in the workplace where people are driven by work plans, deadlines, and contracts.

You could have students create their own contracts from scratch, or give them a template, or provide a completed version they just need to read, discuss and sign. A sample Project Team Contract is included in **Useful Stuff**.

PROJECT TEAM CONTRACT AND TEMPLATE   **✱USE THIS**
(*page 138, 139*)

The other key tool to provide students is a form for planning their work. Typically this is composed of a list of tasks, followed by checkpoints and due dates, then who is responsible — the whole team or individual team members. A sample Project Team Work Plan is included in **Useful Stuff**. Show students how to fill out the Work Plan. You could if you wish lead the whole class in reviewing the project calendar and filling in checkpoints and due dates on their work plans. For young students, much of the information should be filled out by the teacher — for example, they might only decide who will do what on a list of tasks and deadlines provided by you.

K-2 How-to

Re-Teach Teamwork Every Time They Do It

Young children will need a mini-lesson every time they resume working in teams. Model their task and give clear direction before they get started, even if it's the same task as the day before.

PROJECT TEAM WORK PLAN (*page 140*)   **✱USE THIS**

 **Bulletin Board**

Fishbowl Modeling of Collaboration and Other Skills

The fishbowl modeling process can be used to teach many different skills, from how to give each other feedback on a rough draft, to how to share aloud their research notes, to how to self-assess their work as a team. The basic idea is to have one group model the use of a skill while the rest of the class watches what happens in the "fishbowl." Follow the procedure below, which uses collaboration skills as an example.

Preparation:

- On the day before, decide what skill(s) you're going to model, for example: "listening actively," "building on someone else's ideas," "arriving at consensus to make decisions," or "assigning tasks to team members."

- On the day before, identify a team of 3-4 students to participate in the fishbowl. Teach them how to model the skill and have them practice.

- On the day of the fishbowl, have the participants sit in the middle of the room. The other students, the observers, should sit in a larger circle around the students in the fishbowl. You may give everyone a rubric for assessing the skill, or display it.

Directions:

1. Discuss the skill that will be modeled during the fishbowl. Refer to the criteria in the rubric for assessing the skill.

2. Describe what will the fishbowl participants will do to model the skill.

3. Explain the role of the observers during the fishbowl:

   ▶ Observers are not allowed to speak until the debriefing after the fishbowl.

   ▶ Look for evidence that the fishbowl participants are demonstrating the skill.

4. Conduct the fishbowl modeling session.

5. Debrief with the larger group, referring to the rubric, and allow the observers to make comments, report evidence they observed, and ask questions. Ask participants to share what they did and felt.

6. Move students into teams and have them apply the skill in a project task.

Step Three: Manage student teams during the project.

Monitor and coach student teams continually during your project. There are many ways to do this informally. Walk around observing and listening, offering guidance and assistance when students need it. Sit with each team regularly, giving more attention to those that need more support. If needed, remind students about the expectations the class discussed about how to work well in teams, and/or refer to the collaboration rubric.

To monitor and coach teams in more structured ways, remind students to use their Project Work Plans to note their progress on completing project tasks. Look these over regularly, taking action if teams are behind in their work or otherwise having difficulty. To check on how well teams are working together — every few days, or every day if you think it's necessary — you can talk with younger students and have older students write in a journal, or complete a quick survey. Ask questions such as:

- "What is working well in your team?"

- "Is your team having any trouble?"

- "Can you give me an example of a time when someone in your team helped another member in the team?"

- (Upper elementary) "Let's take a look at your team contract. Can you tell me about your progress in honoring your team's norms?"

- (Upper elementary) "What are your team's goals for tomorrow?"

TIPS FROM THE CLASSROOM

Keep the Driving Question in Students' Minds

The DQ is not just announced on Day One and then forgotten. It should be thought about throughout a project. Reflecting on it is a great way to promote students' critical thinking and problem solving skills, and check their evolving understanding of concepts. Keep the DQ alive by:

- Posting it in the room and discussing it with students regularly.

- Explicitly linking lessons and activities to it.

- Having students write in journals about how they would answer it, at various points in the project.

- Revisiting it at the conclusion of the project, noting how it was answered, perhaps in different ways by different students and teams.

An additional structured process for monitoring teams is to have class discussions at regular checkpoints, asking students share their successes and challenges, problem-solving together if necessary. Finally, some PBL teachers schedule meetings with team representatives — and not always those in the formal role of leader — to find out how they're doing. Ask, "Is everyone doing their fair share of the work?" If patterns of difficulty emerge from these meetings or class discussions, you should take the time to reinforce collaboration skills or adjust project tasks and timelines. Or, if only one or a few teams are struggling, work with them separately to get them back on track.

Teaching Students How to Think Critically

In this book we can only scratch the surface of what is involved in teaching students to be good critical thinkers and problem solvers. Entire books and sets of curriculum materials have been written and developed on the topic, especially in recent years. See some recommendations in the Bulletin Board on page 103. Critical thinking and problem solving in PBL is part of BIE's ongoing research and development effort, so keep checking **bie.org** for new ideas and tools.

Remember how we defined critical thinking in the *Getting Started* chapter. It includes defining problems accurately, raising relevant questions, and gathering and evaluating information. It involves analyzing and synthesizing information to support conclusions, while considering alternatives and implications. By design, PBL promotes critical thinking. Well-designed projects present students with tasks that are open-ended, which means the "right answers" are not obvious. Projects involve exploring a topic and creating products that require students to ask questions to guide inquiry, find and use information from various sources, and defend their work when presenting to a public audience.

You might be thinking, "That's a pretty tall order for my first graders. They're going to need a big scaffold to reach that high!" You're right, but think of it this way: Becoming a good critical thinker takes many years (and some people never get there) so your job now is to provide your students, at their level, with a few tools and opportunities to practice. To provide adequate scaffolding for this kind of work, you'll need to use a combination of informal and formal strategies, similar to what you use for collaboration skills.

Bulletin Board | Bloom's Taxonomy for the 21st Century

You may be familiar with Bloom's Taxonomy, a hierarchy of thinking skills first presented by Benjamin Bloom in 1956. Below is a new version proposed in 2001.*

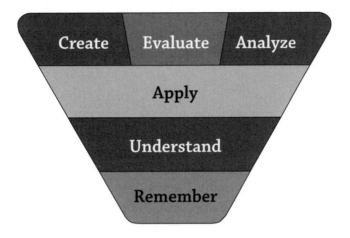

The following example uses the story of Goldilocks and the Three Bears to show what students might do at each level of the new hierarchy. Notice how the highest levels sound like the kind of task or product you'd find in PBL:

- **Remember:** Describe where Goldilocks lived.

- **Understand:** Summarize what the Goldilocks story was about.

- **Apply:** Construct a theory as to why Goldilocks went into the house.

- **Analyze:** Differentiate between how Goldilocks reacted and how you would react in each story event.

- **Evaluate:** Assess whether or not you think this really happened to Goldilocks.

- **Create:** Compose a song, skit, poem, or rap to convey the Goldilocks story in a new form.

A Taxonomy for Learning, Teaching, and Assessing: A Revision of Bloom's Taxonomy of Educational Objectives, 2nd Ed., Allyn & Bacon 2000

Write Critical Thinking Skills in Student-Friendly Language

The following are based on the success skills list on page 31 in the *Getting Started* chapter. Create a list like this that sounds right for your students, post it on the wall, and refer to it when coaching them.

K-2 version:	Upper Elementary version:
I listen.	I can explain a concept, idea or problem in my own words.
I ask questions. 	When my team is discussing a topic or problem, I ask questions that help me understand better.
	I take time to understand a topic or problem before I try to solve it.
I share ideas. 	I use information to help me understand a topic or solve a problem.
I use information. 	I can explain why my conclusions or solutions make sense.
	If one solution to a problem doesn't work, I try another.
I think hard. 	I can explain how different people might look at an issue, problem, or event.

Helping Students Understand what Critical Thinking Means

At the beginning of the project, talk with your students about the kind of thinking that's required. How sophisticated this discussion is depends on their age, of course, but let students know they're going to need to "think hard" and "ask good questions" and "explain how your ideas make sense." Give some examples.

Your students will find it helpful if you make the abstract concept of critical thinking more concrete and specific. Break it down for them by giving them a student-friendly list of indicators of critical thinking. Then ask them to explain in their own words what it looks and sounds like in practice. See the example on the *Bulletin Board* on page 100.

One of the best ways to teach students what critical thinking skills are is to model them, using the "think-aloud" strategy to make your thought process transparent for students. Basically, a think-aloud is an internal conversation that you make public while approaching and working through a task. The students hear the internal dialog and see the use of critical thinking skills modeled by the teacher. You can keep track of your think-aloud conversation visually, using chart paper or a white board, or use a Smart Board or other technology.

Let's look at two examples from our Spotlight Projects that show how a teacher can model critical thinking.

In the second grade "Pizza and the World of Work" project, Laurel would pause regularly after the children learned something about the world of work, from their reading or from interviewing people.

- *To model how "good thinkers" ask questions she said things like, "What questions do I have about _____ now?" then listed a few.*

- *To model how good thinkers use information, she asked, "How can I find out more about this before I decide what I think?" then offered ideas about other people she could talk with.*

- *To model how good thinkers compare ideas, she asked "How does what it says in this book compare to what it says in _____?" then gave a few possible answers.*

- *To model the use of evidence to support a conclusion, she said "I think the job of _____ is harder than _____" then explained how she would back up her reasoning.*

In the fifth grade "Selling a Cell" project the students' task was to choose a cell phone plan. Gina didn't want them to copy her, so she decided to use a comparable example and modeled how she would choose which new car to buy. She wrote and drew on the whiteboard as she modeled, putting things in categories and drawing lines to connect them. Breaking down the process, she:

1. *Explained the problem in her own words, to be sure she understood it.*

2. *Identified her needs, wants, and resources, such as, "What do I use a car for?" and "What kind of car and features do I like?" and "How much can I spend?" then listed some answers to these questions.*

3. *Identified information needs, asking "What do I need to find out?" She listed items such as gas mileage, cost, loans available, and the trade-in value of her old car.*

4. *Identified sources of information, asking, "How could I find answers to my questions?" and wrote some ideas.*

5. *Considered the quality of the information, asking, "But how will I know what they tell me is true?" and said, "I'd better compare at least two or three sources of information!"*

*Gina returned to this story at another key point during the project, to model how to put information together and use it to draw a conclusion. She reminded her students that explaining **why** a conclusion makes sense is an important part of critical thinking, and provided a justification for her decision. After she was done with the think-aloud, she asked students to offer feedback about whether her conclusion was correct and her justification was convincing.*

Providing Students with Tools

To help students be effective critical thinkers and problem solvers during a project, give them tools such as:

- Graphic organizers (bubble maps to show connections between brainstormed ideas, flowcharts to show a sequence of ideas or steps, branching diagrams to show how ideas or topics lead to others)

- A list of thinking, writing, and discussion starters students can use when working in teams (such as, "I think the problem is basically about..." "Can you explain that in another way? Can you give me an example?" and "My idea makes sense because...")

- Step-by-step protocols for approaching a problem (e.g., "1. Explain it. 2. Ask questions about it. 3. Get information. 4. Try different solutions. 5. Decide which solution is best.")

Coaching Students During the Project

During a project, many opportunities arise for coaching students to be good critical thinkers and problem solvers. Informally, ask them to explain their thinking as you move around the room or lead a discussion. Refer to a poster or other tool you might have provided that describes good thinking or lists steps for approaching a problem.

More formal opportunities for coaching these skills occur during writer's and reader's workshops, where you can ask students to be clear and accurate, use evidence, be logical, and consider alternative ideas. Use peer assessment critique protocols (like the one described by Ron Berger in the Bulletin Board on page 107) that encourage students to be good thinkers.

Generally speaking, you can build students' thinking and problem solving skills during a project by:

- Allowing students to find their own solution, even if in your view it is not perfect

- Looking for opportunities for brainstorming

- Comparing and contrasting (everything from objects and facts to ideas and products)

- Categorizing (everything from objects and questions to facts and ideas)

- Encouraging creativity (along with evaluation of the quality of an idea or product)

- Requiring students to always use evidence when making decisions

(Adapted from "Critical Thinking in the Elementary Classroom: Problems and Solutions" by Vera Schneider, 2002 Educators Publishing Service)

TIPS FROM THE **CLASSROOM**

Find Critical Thinking on the Web

If you search "critical thinking" you'll get dozens of websites. Most are selling books, posters, and lessons that teach skills such as logic and reasoning, often using puzzles and brain teasers. While these are valuable skills, we believe they should be taught in the context of a project, not only as isolated exercises.

Here are some resources that PBL teachers recommend:

- **ThinkingMaps.com** is one of the best online sources of graphic organizers, with templates for diagrams, maps, columned charts, flowcharts, and so on.

- **tc2.ca** from The Critical Thinking Consortium is an excellent resource for K-12 teachers of all subjects.

- **criticalthinking.org** from The Foundation for Critical Thinking offers an extensive set of materials, workshops, and research.

- **creativelearning.com** from the Center for Creative Learning, Inc. emphasizes creativity and problem-solving.

Using Formative Assessment and Setting Checkpoints

Just like going to the dentist for regular check-ups prevents cavities, formative assessment is one of the most important practices for improving learning in any classroom. In a PBL environment, it's even more important to check students' understanding and monitor their progress. During a multi-week project in which students need to understand a topic in depth and create high-quality products, working independently from the teacher some of the time, you need to make sure students are "getting it" as well as getting it done.

Purposes of Formative Assessment in PBL

The basic reason for using formative assessment, of course, is to see if you need to provide additional support to students or intervene if they are getting off track in a project. You don't want to spend the time PBL requires if learning goals are not being met, or show student work to a public audience if it's not of high quality.

During your project, use formative assessment for two purposes:

- To find out if students have the content knowledge, understanding, and skills they need to answer the Driving Question and create major products.

- To check the quality and progress of products that students create — from the initial stages to final versions — as they develop their answer to the Driving Question and prepare to present their work to an audience.

TIPS FROM THE **CLASSROOM**

Create a Culture of Critique and Revision

Formative assessment works best if it's part of a collaborative culture you establish among your students, focused on producing high-quality work. Through your words and actions, make it safe for students to reflect honestly and openly about their successes and failures. Tell them, "It's OK to make mistakes, that's how we learn!"

One on the best books on this topic is:

An Ethic of Excellence: Building a Culture of Craftsmanship with Students

by Ron Berger (Heinemann, 2003).

Guide Students in Self-Assessment

One important attribute of PBL is that the assessment process is a shared process. During a project, even young students can monitor their own progress, along with the teacher and including feedback from peers if appropriate. At the end of a project, provide students an opportunity to assess the quality of their work.

To guide students in assessing their project products:

1. Review the criteria (on a rubric) for evaluating a product or presentation.

2. Using an example, model a "think aloud" strategy to show them how to apply the criteria to a product.

3. Ask them to mark up the rubric, highlighting or circling words that apply, and/or have them write comments on a form (or talk with younger students) to explain their judgment.

4. Provide students with feedback on their self-evaluation, explaining where you agreed with them — or where you did not.

Who Does Formative Assessment in PBL

It's not only the teacher who conducts formative assessment — students should learn how too, since one of the goals of PBL is to teach them how to be independent and take responsibility for their own work. As the teacher, you have the primary responsibility for checking background knowledge and skills, using the various strategies you outlined in the last chapter when you developed your balanced assessment plan. You also provide feedback on the quality and progress of the products students create, but guide them in self and peer assessment too. This helps students learn the skills and habits of critique and revision, which are important lifelong learning skills. Another key reason for using self and peer assessment is that it leads to better quality work because it increases the total amount of feedback students receive — it's more than you as one person can provide. And there's one more aspect to consider: the feedback students get from each other is often very effective in motivating them to improve their work.

How to Do Formative Assessment in PBL

The way you do formative assessment of content knowledge, understanding, and skills during a project is not all that different from what you might already do in non-PBL teaching. You still use a combination of informal and formal methods, from observing and talking with younger students to written assignments, homework, quizzes, and guided practice for older students. Do quick checks using various methods you might already use to see if students understand a concept, such as having them write an answer to a question on paper or small whiteboards. During your project, use these and whatever other methods you have in your toolbox regularly and often.

To formatively assess the quality and progress of the products your students are creating during a project, establish routines and procedures that students come to know and expect, such as:

- Use rubrics or other sets of criteria to show students what they need to do to improve their work and as tools for self- and peer assessment.

- Structure review sessions to focus on a specific aspect or trait of the product. Examine exemplars and assess them as a class, and have students note how they can improve their own work.

- Establish peer review protocols, such as exchanging work-in-progress with other teams, having one team critique its work in a "fishbowl" as the class observes, or conducting a "gallery walk" with student work posted around the room for peers to comment on.

- Submit work-in-progress to outside experts for review, if you use them in your project.

Set Regular Checkpoints on Your Project Calendar

If you haven't done this already during the planning stage, an important part of managing your project is to set deadlines for when students should complete each step in the journey. These checkpoints are occasions for formative assessment — for feedback, critique and reflection. At checkpoints, have students submit artifacts such as research notes, drafts of written work, storyboards for videos, sketches and plans, and models or prototypes of products. Decide what the major milestones are by working backwards from your project's end point. Mark progress on a Project Calendar or other visual aide, noting milestones reached and those that are approaching.

For example, in the "Parkland on Display" Spotlight Project, the fourth graders were presenting their museum exhibits at the end of the sixth week. That meant they needed to have their materials ready to assemble by the end of the fifth

A Protocol for Critique & Revision of Project Products

Bulletin Board

"Students will say that this piece of writing is good because Suzy is a good writer. Teachers need to help students name what is good about Suzy's writing, because once we name it, then we can use it."

— Ron Berger, *Chief Program Officer, Expeditionary Learning*

The following is a protocol suggested by Ron Berger that is useful for formative assessment:

Purpose: To teach particular skills to students. It is not for the whole class to give one student feedback on his or her work.

Critique Rules: 1. Be kind 2. Be specific 3. Be helpful

The Protocol:

1. **The lesson:** Think about what lesson you are trying to teach your students. After looking at drafts of student work, what is the big idea that students are missing? What is troubling about the work? What's the next step that many of the students are ready to take? Try to list 3-6 skills that you want students to get better at.

2. **Selecting the work:** It is most important to find examples of student work that are great examples of what the teacher is looking for from the students, or else great examples of exactly *not* what the teacher is looking for.* Looking at merely mediocre work will not lead to helpful discussion.

3. **The critique:**

   a. Give students one or two pieces of student work for in-depth critique. Examples include excerpts from student writing, plans and proposals, prototypes or models, solutions to problems, science activity write-ups, etc.

   b. Allow students time to look silently at the work and think about what makes the work high-quality or where it fall short. Depending on age level, students could be given time to discuss this in small groups.

   c. Lead a group conversation about the work. The goal is to identify the attributes of great student work for this particular assignment. Once those attributes are *identified*, they need to be *named* in simple kid language so that they can be *used* by kids. Coach students toward the 3-6 skills identified in advance, keeping in mind that students may think of other useful skills that can be named.

4. **Next draft:** Students now create a new draft of this assignment, incorporating the skills identified during the critique session. It is helpful if students know in advance that a particular assignment in going to be completed in (say) three drafts. It is helpful if each draft is somewhat different from the one that came before it to avoid student burnout on a particular draft. For example, students could graduate to making an architectural drawing on a nicer type of paper with each succeeding draft. Or the first draft could be a rough sketch of a storyboard. The next draft could be a detailed sketch of the storyboard. The next draft could be a polished storyboard with audio tracks written, like those used by professionals in the field.

*Note: If you use an example of low-quality work, it is important to use work done by a student who your students don't know. Remove the student's name from the work sample if it appears.

week, and written plans and sketches for the exhibit done by the end of the fourth week, and their research notes done by the end of the third week. And they needed to practice their oral presentations during the first two days of the sixth week. Reaching these milestones, with time for feedback and revision, allowed the students — and their teachers — to feel ready for the big show. In the "Creatures of Oldham County" project, the kindergarteners, with Abbey's help, needed to have the text written for their book on the third Friday, the week before the book was assembled and presented, and have their research questions answered by the second Friday. (See the sample Project Calendar on page 149, 150.)

Preparing for and Facilitating Presentations to an Audience

The presentation is one of the most essential components of a project, so it is important to provide adequate time and attention to prepare your students. Children — like most adults — often fear the challenge of speaking in front of large groups. However, the more support that you provide, the more confident they will be. Students will need explicit instruction regarding how to organize and deliver their presentations and how to field questions from the audience. The expectations regarding presentation skills varies widely across grade levels, so review your state standards to see if the expectations are outlined for your grade level.

How Will Students Interact with People Who See Their Work?

Before you can prepare for presentations, you need to envision what it will be like when your students meet their audience. They should not simply present their work, but also interact in some way with other people. Even if students are simply standing next to something they've created, and not actually making a formal presentation, make sure they talk with people who've come to see it. Or if students have posted their work online (e.g., created a website or blog for students in distance places to see) or distributed it to others (e.g., a brochure for a group in the community), at least have them collect feedback from those who see it. Ask for viewers or readers to post questions, offer comments, or take a survey.

For some projects, you might ask audience members to play a role when asking questions. For example, they might pretend they are the clients for whom students have developed a product or performed a service, or stakeholders hearing proposals on an issue.

If students are presenting to a live audience, you and audience members should ask questions. This is another way for students to show they learned the content and can think critically and use problem solving skills. The number of questions, and how challenging they are, depends on the age of your students. You can ask questions about what they know, and also about the process they used to complete the project. Have them explain the choices they made, describe processes they used, and make connections and predictions. A question-and-answer session can also be a key part of your assessment.

To Prepare Students for Presentations:

- Make sure students understand the goals of the presentation and the rubric for it.

- Have students watch video clips or live demonstrations of strong, interesting presentations, and a few weaker ones (as long as they don't know the people in them, or it's done intentionally by a teacher in a live demonstration!). Critique the presentations using a rubric or by generating a list of criteria on an "anchor chart" to refer back to.

- Teach students how to organize their ideas for the presentation. A planning form or template is helpful — see the one provided in *Useful Stuff*.

Questioning Children During Presentations

Use your judgment about asking young children questions when they present — and give guidelines to audience members. Keep questions short and simple. Focus on knowledge, not complex critical thinking skills. If a student is nervous or doesn't seem to understand a question, don't press too hard.

PRESENTATION PLANNING FORM (*page 141*)   **✳ USE THIS**

- If appropriate for your grade level, help students shape their presentations based on the audience, the information that they need to communicate, and the setting.

- Create an environment in which students feel comfortable providing feedback to one another using the presentation rubric while practicing their presentations.

- Schedule practice presentations with enough time for feedback and revisions if needed.

- Provide opportunities for students to build their confidence by presenting to increasingly larger groups, from individual peers, to small groups, to the entire class, to a small group from the community, to a larger group that includes a panel.

Also remember the importance of content knowledge in PBL. When students thoroughly understand the concepts underlying the project topic, their confidence level rises. Everything that you do to build their background knowledge about the topic will make students more prepared for their presentations. You'll find that even young students have an easier time presenting about a topic learned through an interesting, in-depth investigation, as opposed to regurgitating facts learned by memorization.

Before Presentation Day: Be Prepared Yourself

If you planned your project thoroughly and arranged your resources before it started, the logistics — schedule, facilities, equipment, and personnel — should not be an issue on presentation day. But just to help make sure you've got everything ready, we've provided a checklist in the back of this book.

✳ USE THIS PRESENTATION DAY CHECKLIST (*page 142*)

TIPS FROM THE CLASSROOM

Prepare Your Audience for Complex Duties

If the audience or panel members for presentations will be play-acting a role that will be somewhat demanding, explain it to them thoroughly. If they are acting as active assessors of student work, they'll also need advance preparation. Send key documents and coach them via phone calls, email, online postings, or perhaps by meeting with them. If they're going to be using a rubric, it definitely would be best to meet with them ahead of time to explain how to use it.

On Presentation Day: How to Wear Two Hats

Hat #1: Host with the Most

Wear this hat if any guests are coming into your classroom, and especially when community members or parents are visiting the school. You'll need to put on your meet-and-greet face to welcome them, making sure they know where to sit and where the refreshments and restrooms are. You can also employ students as greeters who perform these duties.

Inform your audience about what they should do:

- If the audience is going to be passive — simply watching and listening but not asking probing questions or evaluating the presenters — just tell them what to expect, whether they should ask questions, and when to break into wild applause.

- If presentations are to be kept to a strict time limit, let the presenters and audience know that you might be giving signals to wrap it up or cut short a question session.

- If you think a student audience needs a reminder about "how to be a good audience," give it.

- If the audience is playing a more active, complex role for which they have been prepared, give them just a quick reminder.

You may want to give your audience some handouts:

- a written summary of the project

- a list of sample questions to ask (about both content and process, if you wish)

- a form for recording their feedback and comments

PRESENTATION AUDIENCE FEEDBACK FORM   **✱ USE THIS**
(*page 143*)

Hat #2: Keen-Eyed, Sharp-Eared Assessor

Wear this hat once the presentations begin. Put your rubric(s) in front of you, make sure you can see and hear well, then get ready to pay close attention. If you're making a video recording of the presentations, you can refer to it later to help you remember and assess, but that takes time. Get as much done as you can during the live action.

Ideally, you should assess your students while observing and listening as *other* people ask questions and probe their understanding and knowledge. If others are asking questions, even stock questions you provided, you are free to focus 100% of your attention on what your students say and do. If you are the only one with the expertise to ask certain questions, you may need to join in, but try to step back and watch as much as possible.

Here are some suggestions of questions you could ask — of upper elementary students, although for younger children you could modify them — following a presentation:

If you want to find out:	Ask questions such as:
If students really understand a concept, or whether they have just memorized some words to say	▸ Can you explain that in another way?
Students' depth and breadth of knowledge of a topic	▸ Can you give me some more facts about that? ▸ Could you give me more examples?
If students can correctly use new or technical vocabulary	▸ Can you tell me what that means?
If students can think critically and make connections from their topic to other issues	▸ Could you connect that with _____? ▸ How would someone react to _____ if they were _____?
How and why students did what they did in the project	▸ Could you tell me how you found that information? ▸ How did you reach that conclusion or find that solution? ▸ What other ideas did you consider? ▸ What were the biggest challenges? ▸ What questions are you still wondering about?

TIPS FROM THE **CLASSROOM**

Keep the Other Students Busy While a Group is Presenting

A common question teachers ask about managing a project is, "What do I do with the rest of the class during presentations?" Here are some ideas:

- Teach students how to be a good audience, then remind them. Repeat as often as necessary.

- If appropriate for your grade level, give them a task, such as taking notes on key points or strong arguments; writing down questions to ask afterward; scoring each other on a rubric or checklist.

- If you have reasons for not wanting students to see another group's presentation beforehand, arrange to put them in two separate rooms, if possible. Once students present, they can become audience members for groups that follow.

- Have students assess themselves after their presentation by filling out a rubric and writing comments.

REFLECTING AND PERFECTING

This Chapter's Goal

Whew. Almost there—time for the last phase of your project, after the presentations are over and major products have been collected. In this chapter we'll explain how to reflect upon what was learned and improve your project by:

- Celebrating Success

- Guiding Student Reflection about What Was Learned

- Gathering Feedback from Students about the Project

- Using Data to Plan for Re-Teaching and to Improve Your Project

- Saving Examples of Student Work and Project Artifacts

We'll end with a final reflection from BIE.

Why "Reflect" After a Project Ends?

Taking the time to reflect on a project is a last step that often gets overlooked, but it's important for several reasons. Reflection helps students retain what they learn, because they go over it one more time in their minds, connecting it to what they already know and to other topics and ideas. Revisiting the Driving Question and the key concepts in the project helps them sink in deeper. The last step of a project is also a good time for students to assess how well they collaborated with their peers and used other success skills as they look back on the process they used to learn and complete tasks. Finally, discussing the project with students, and noting your own thoughts about it while they're fresh, can help you improve your project and plan for the next one. So after the big finish, when the presentations are over and the products completed, allow yourself and your students some time to think about what you've been through.

There's another reason to include time to reflect when you plan your project calendar. It has to do with the emotional experience of doing of PBL. After a lengthy, challenging, and (you hope) rewarding and exciting experience together, a group should recognize the significance of what it has accomplished. If your project ended with whiz-bang presentations to an audience on Friday, wouldn't it somehow feel wrong on Monday to just move on to the next unit without a look back? A project should strike students as being different from traditional instruction. So use thoughtful reflection time to drive home that realization—and make them look forward to their next project.

> After a lengthy, challenging, rewarding and exciting experience together, a group should recognize the significance of what it has accomplished.

OK, let's consider how to properly wrap up your project!

Celebrating Success

Along with reflection at the end of the project, don't forget the celebration. This is another aspect of PBL that mirrors what happens in the world outside of school, where it's common to celebrate the completion of good work. Office workers go out to dinner, politicians cut ceremonial ribbons, nurses and doctors hug patients and salespeople high-five their boss. Sports provide lots of examples, such as when athletes parade down Main Street and trophies are awarded. The completion of a project in a classroom should be no different. The celebration can be formal or informal.

Ways to Celebrate a Project

■ Invite audience members to stay around after presentations for a reception, to talk informally with students and offer praise.

■ Invite school and/or district administrators who were aware of the project, or outside experts, community members and parents who were involved, to visit your classroom and offer congratulations.

■ In a whole-class activity, tell your students how proud you are of their accomplishments, with specific examples. Then ask them to create their own list of "What We Are Proud Of."

■ Let your community know. Get a local reporter for a newspaper, radio or TV station to cover your project and tout the results. Arrange for project work to be displayed at a local government office, business, public library, museum, gallery, community center, etc.

■ Create an archive or "memorial" of some kind. Students could create a display of their work, contribute words or phrases to a signed "The ____ Project Was…" poster to go on the classroom wall, assemble images and writing in a scrapbook, or place project artifacts in online archive. These memorials could be kept with pride all year, shown to parents, visitors, administrators and colleagues, and to other students as helpful examples of what good PBL looks like. (See page 121-122 for more tips on saving samples of student work.)

Guiding Student Reflection about What Was Learned

As soon as possible after the project's culminating presentations and after all the products have been turned in, ask your students to look back on the journey they've completed. But before you decide on *what* to ask them, decide on the *process* you'll use to have students reflect. We recommend a combination of individual, small group, and whole-class methods.

Methods for Student Reflection

■ Individual journal entry, a set of written responses, or a survey on a form you create (like the one in *Useful Stuff*)

SELF-REFLECTION ON THE PROJECT FORM
(*page 144*)

✱USE THIS

Polish Up that Reflectivity

Students may not see the value of reflection, and many will not know how or tend to answer questions quickly and without much thought. To counteract this tendency, here are three ideas:

- Jump-start the process by having students discuss questions with a partner or in small groups, then write individual reflections

- Provide an example of what a thoughtful comment looks like

- When a student shares a well-thought out reflection with the class, point out what was specifically good about it: "I appreciate the thoughtfulness of Tony's reflection! He said, …"

- Think-Pair-Share, in which individuals think about and perhaps jot down a response to questions you provide, share it with a partner, then contribute to a whole-class discussion. Record comments for everyone to see.

- Small group discussion, followed by whole-class. Record comments for everyone to see.

- Fishbowl discussion, in which each group sends a representative to the front of the room to sit in a circle to discuss the project as the class listens. You can leave an "open chair" for any class member to pop in with a comment, then pop out. Record comments for everyone to see.

What Students Can Reflect On

You should adapt these questions — or think of your own — according to your own style, your project, and what's appropriate for your students' age and readiness. But here are some ideas for the kinds of questions you can ask about:

The Project's Major Tasks and Big Ideas

- How good were the product(s) you created? What could have been improved?

- What is the best solution to the problem we were solving, and why? What other solutions might make sense?

- What is your answer to the Driving Question now? Did your thinking about it change during the project? (Note: This applies mainly to the second type of DQ described on page 40, one that focuses on an issue or big idea rather than a product).

- What does this project make you wonder about, or want to learn more about?

What They Learned in Terms of Academic Content and Skills

- What did you learn about _____? (It's OK to start with a general question like this, to see what they got out of it. You can add more specific questions.)

- What skills did you get better at? (e.g., reading, writing, using math, researching, etc. — ask for specific examples.)

What They Learned in Terms of Success Skills

Collaboration:

- How did you work as a team? What would have made you work better as a team?

- How good a team member were you? What did you do well, and what could you improve?

- Did you do your work on time? Were you organized? What would you do differently next time?

Communication:

- How well did you use presentation skills? What could you have improved?

- Did you think about who your audience was when you showed them your work? How did this affect your presentation?

Critical Thinking/Problem Solving:

- Explain how you really had to think hard about something during the project.

- Describe an example of how you solved a problem in the project.

- If things went wrong during the project, how did you respond?

 Helping Children Assess Success Skills

Young students may not able to step back and evaluate how well they worked on a team or thought critically, especially if you want them to think back over a lengthy project. This can be challenging even for older students and adults.

Schedule time to talk with students individually. Review what it means to be a good team member or to think critically and be a good problem solver. Look over a rubric together and browse through a project journal or portfolio to look for evidence that the student met the criteria or just talk about some examples. Then, collaboratively fill out the rubric.

Take that Last Chance to Correct Misunderstandings

When students offer comments on what they have learned, you may notice that they still don't quite understand a concept or a process completely. You may, in fact, want to ask some probing questions during the reflection phase to make sure that your content goals were accomplished. Maybe they're misusing a key term, or not seeing the connection between what they learned and its application to something else. You might have picked up on this misunderstanding when students' work was on display too, despite your best efforts to catch it in advance by providing formative feedback. And it may have been obvious from your assessment of their work that students simply didn't fully "get" something important.

If this happens, take the time while the moment is ripe to clarify their thinking. If it's only a few students, you could talk or work with them separately, but if it's many, act now with the whole class. Even if it means taking more time than you planned, this is one of those "teachable moments" when students are most ready to learn. You don't want them to leave the project with erroneous ideas or superficial understanding.

Gathering Feedback from Students about the Project

After a project ends you will have your own sense of its strengths and weaknesses, but don't forget to ask your students for their thoughts. They may see the project very differently. Students might have experienced things or have a point of view that you did not see or realize. And, students' opinions matter in PBL — they were not just passive recipients of your teaching, but active partners on the journey. In other words, they *deserve* a chance to contribute ideas for improving the project. And there's a third reason you might need to remember especially if your project did not go as well as you hoped: students might point out good things which you didn't notice.

You can use the same methods for gathering feedback that we described above on pages 115-116. Ask your students questions such as the suggestions below, or use the form we've provided in *Useful Stuff*.

SELF-REFLECTION ON THE PROJECT FORM **✳USE THIS**
(*page 144*)

Questions to Ask Students about a Project's Design

- Was the project interesting, challenging in a good way, fun?

- Did you feel like you were doing things that people in the real world do?

- Was the project too simple, too complicated, or just right? Why?

- Do you feel like you did important work in the project?

Questions to Ask Students about a Project's Implementation:

- Was it the right length of time?

- Were the instructions clear?

- What were the biggest challenges?

- Did you get the right amount of help from me/the teacher?

- Did I/the teacher let you make some choices about what to do?

- Did you need more help with something during the project?

A Simple Way to Gather Feedback

Instead of asking young children to provide detailed answers to several questions, have a class discussion. Draw a two-column chart headed, "I Liked" and "I Didn't Like" and record their thoughts.

Using Data to Plan for Re-Teaching and to Improve Your Project

We've said it before—a project is a journey that can be exciting, challenging, rewarding, and downright fun. But when the journey ends, after the celebration and the thoughtful reflections, remember to ask the BIG question: Did we get where we intended to go? You specified several goals when you designed the project, so use the data you've collected to analyze the results of your project with a clear, unblinking eye. Then use the data to plan action and improve the project for next time.

Sources of data about student achievement in a project

There are several sources of evidence you should look at when deciding how well your goals were met:

- Your own observations as students worked

- Your analysis of major products and performances, including how they compare to previous work your students have done

- Comments from other adults who served as resources or mentors, or who saw major products and performances

- Completed assessment rubrics

- Students' self-reports and reflections

- Tests and quizzes, if applicable

What to do if the data reveal a shortfall in student achievement

The decision you need to make now is, "Do I need to re-teach something, and when?" Use this basic process:

- Make note of which standards (knowledge, understanding, and skills) were not learned well enough.

- Decide if the standards should be re-taught immediately, using other methods besides PBL, or whether they could be included in a future project.

- Make note of which success skills, or which aspects of them, were not being used effectively.

- Decide if, when, and how certain success skills should be emphasized in future projects.

Using the data to improve your project

After you've analyzed your data and asked students their opinion, it's time to sum it all up. Perhaps you have a mind like a steel trap and will remember exactly how you thought the project could be improved the next time you run it. But perhaps you will get caught up in the next rush of events in your classroom and school, and the details will get a little fuzzy. And when you dust off the project file next year, you'll find yourself saying, "Oh yeah, what was that major problem with the rubric again?"

To guard against this possibility, we've provided — guess what? — a handy form you can use to record your reflections on several aspects of your project.

TEACHER'S POST-PROJECT REVIEW FORM
(*page 145, 146*)

✳ USE THIS

Saving Examples of Student Work and Project Artifacts

Wait! Don't return all their work to students before you save some examples. Although students might bring their project work home proudly or stash it in their desks until June, they're just as likely to trash it and you'll never be able to see it again. And don't you trash it yet either, much as you might need the space in your classroom, file drawer, or computer. You will find that keeping some examples of student work from your project is good idea. You don't need to save *all* student work — just key examples that illustrate what happened during the project, and examples of finished products that represent the range of quality you received. Why bother saving student work? Here are some reasons:

- When you do the project again, you can use examples of student work to show students what they're being asked to do. Good work can "raise the bar" and motivate students.

Student Work Samples at Expeditionary Learning

One of the best places to see examples of student work from projects is a showcase on the website of Expeditionary Learning, a K-12 school reform organization the emphasizes PBL. Each example of a product created by students is linked to a description of the project that led to it. See it at:

modelsofexcellence.eleducation.org/projects

- Analyzing samples of high, medium, and low quality work will help you write or revise rubrics so they capture your expectations in clear, specific, descriptive language.

- Student work samples give students a concrete idea of what you expect them to accomplish. Have them critique the samples using a rubric, to make clear the specific criteria for high-quality work.

- You never know when someone may ask you to describe your project, and samples of student work tell a powerful story. You can show student work at Back-to-School Night or other events involving parents, or use it at conferences and other professional development events or when working with colleagues and administrators.

Student work to save:

- Video recordings (with good audio quality!) of presentations

- Copies of media produced: video, slides, web pages, audio recordings

- Photographs of displays, exhibits, posters, models, works of art

- Copies of written products (electronic and/or paper)

Other materials from the project to save:

- Websites, books, organizations, community members, and other resources that proved useful

- Concept maps, research notes, interview logs

- Rough drafts, prototypes, field work notes

Concluding Reflections from BIE

That's all for now, folks. We hope you're ready to get out there and do some wonderful projects with your students. We know PBL takes hard work, like any effective teaching method, on the part of people like you. But after a successful project you'll know it was worth it!

Please let us know if you have any questions, suggestions, or stories to tell. Our website, **bie.org**, has a Forum where you can post questions about PBL and get answers from BIE staff and other educators. Also on our site you'll find videos of projects in action, a Do It Yourself project design tutorial, and a Project Search tool. If you or someone you know is interested in PBL professional development, support for an organization, or research, you know where to go.

Remember to check **bie.org** now and then for updated materials to download, including what you find here in *Useful Stuff*. We'll also post additional materials we create and receive from people — like you? — in classrooms around the U.S. and the world. Stay in touch.

Other Books about PBL in ES

If you'd like to see what other authors say about doing projects in elementary school, here are three we'd recommend, all of which focus on children in the early elementary and even pre-K years:

Engaging Children's Minds: the Project Approach
By Lilian G. Katz and Sylvia C. Chard
(Praeger; 2nd edition, 2000)

Young Investigators: the Project Approach in the Early Years
By Judy Harris Helm and Lilian Katz
(Teachers College Press, 2001)

Project-Based Learning with Young Children
By Deborah Diffily and Charlotte Sassman
(Heinemann, 2002)

USEFUL STUFF

Tools for Planning and Managing a Project

(You can also download them and find updated versions from **bie.org**.)

continued

Examples of Completed Forms and Other Materials:

PROJECT DESIGN: OVERVIEW

Name of Project:		Duration:
Subject/Course:	Teacher(s):	Grade Level:
Other subject areas to be included, if any:		

Key Knowledge and Understanding (CCSS or other standards)		
Success Skills (to be taught and assessed)	Critical Thinking/Problem Solving	Self-Management
	Collaboration	Other:
Project Summary (include student role, issue, problem or challenge, action taken, and purpose/beneficiary)		
Driving Question		
Entry Event		
Products	Individual:	Specific content and competencies to be assessed:
	Team:	Specific content and competencies to be assessed:

Making Products Public (include how the products will be made public and who students will engage with during/at end of project)

Resources Needed

On-site people, facilities:

Equipment:

Materials:

Community Resources:

Reflection Methods (how individual, team, and/or whole class will reflect during/at end of project)

Journal/Learning Log	Focus Group
Whole-Class Discussion	Fishbowl Discussion
Survey	Other:

Notes:

PROJECT DESIGN: STUDENT LEARNING GUIDE

Project:

Driving Question:

Final Product(s) Presentations, Performances, Products and/or Services	Learning Outcomes/Targets knowledge, understanding & success skills needed by students to successfully complete products	Checkpoints/Formative Assessments to check for learning and ensure students are on track	Instructional Strategies for All Learners provided by teacher, other staff, experts; includes scaffolds, materials, lessons aligned to learning outcomes and formative assessments
(individual **and** team)			

PROJECT CALENDAR

page 1

Project:

Time Frame:

	MONDAY	TUESDAY	WEDNESDAY	THURSDAY	FRIDAY
PROJECT WEEK ONE					
Notes					
PROJECT WEEK TWO					
Notes					

Project:

MONDAY	TUESDAY	WEDNESDAY	THURSDAY	FRIDAY

PROJECT WEEK THREE

Notes

PROJECT WEEK FOUR

Notes

	Below Standard	Approaching Standard	At Standard	Above Standard ✓
Explanation of Ideas & Information	▸ uses inappropriate facts and irrelevant details to support main ideas	▸ chooses some facts and details that support main ideas, but there may not be enough, or some are irrelevant	▸ chooses appropriate facts and relevant, descriptive details to support main ideas and themes	
Organization	▸ does not include everything required in presentation ▸ presents ideas in an order that does not make sense ▸ does not plan timing of presentation well; it is too short or too long	▸ includes almost everything required in presentation ▸ tries to present ideas in an order, but it doesn't always makes sense ▸ presents for the right length of time, but some parts may be too short or too long	▸ includes everything required in presentation ▸ presents ideas in an order that makes sense ▸ organizes time well; no part of the presentation is rushed, too short or too long	
Eyes & Body	▸ does not look at audience; reads notes ▸ fidgets or slouches a lot	▸ makes some eye contact, but reads notes or slides most of the time ▸ fidgets or slouches a little	▸ keeps eye contact with audience most of the time; only glances at notes or slides ▸ has a confident posture	
Voice	▸ speaks too quietly or not clearly ▸ does not speak appropriately for the situation (may be too informal or use slang)	▸ speaks loudly and clearly most of the time ▸ speaks appropriately for the situation most of the time	▸ speaks loudly and clearly ▸ speaks appropriately for the situation, using formal English when appropriate	
Presentation Aids	▸ does not use audio/visual aids or media ▸ uses inappropriate or distracting audio/visual aids or media	▸ uses audio/visual aids or media, but they sometimes distract from the presentation, or do not add to ideas and themes	▸ uses well-produced audio/visual aids or media to add to main ideas and themes	
Response to Audience Questions	▸ does not answer audience questions	▸ answers some audience questions, but not clearly or completely	▸ answers audience questions clearly and completely	
Participation in Team Presentations	▸ Not all team members participate; only one or two speak	▸ All team members participate, but not equally	▸ All team members participate for about the same length of time, and are able to answer questions	

Presentation Rubric for PBL
(for grades K-2)

I plan a beginning, middle, and end.

1. still learning

2. sometimes

3. almost always

I use pictures, drawings, and props.

1. still learning

2. sometimes

3. almost always

I look at my audience.

1. still learning

2. sometimes

3. almost always

I speak loudly and clearly.

1. still learning

2. sometimes

3. almost always

I answer questions from the audience.

1. still learning

2. sometimes

3. almost always

COLLABORATION RUBRIC for PBL: *Individual Performance*
(for grades 3-5)

	Below Standard	Approaching Standard	At Standard	Above Standard ✔
Takes Responsibility	▸ I need to prepare for and join team discussions ▸ I need reminders to do project work ▸ My project work is not done on time ▸ I need to learn how to use feedback from others	▸ I am usually prepared for and join team discussions ▸ I do some project work, but sometimes need to be reminded ▸ I complete most project work on time ▸ I sometimes use feedback from others	▸ I am prepared for work with the team; I have studied required material and use it to explore ideas in discussions ▸ I do project work without having to be reminded ▸ I complete project work on time ▸ I use feedback from others to improve my work	
Helps the Team	▸ I need to cooperate with my team and help the team solve problems ▸ I need to learn how to help make discussions effective ▸ I need to learn how to give useful feedback to others ▸ I need to learn to offer to help others if they need it	▸ I cooperate with the team but do not help it solve problems ▸ I usually help make discussions effective, but do not always follow the rules, ask enough questions, or express ideas clearly ▸ I give feedback to others, but it may not always be helpful ▸ I sometimes offer to help others if they need it	▸ I help the team solve problems and manage conflicts ▸ I help make discussions effective by following agreed-upon rules, asking and answering questions, clearly expressing ideas ▸ I give helpful feedback to others ▸ I offer to help others do their work if needed	
Respects Others	▸ I am sometimes impolite or unkind to teammates (may interrupt, ignore others' ideas, hurt feelings) ▸ I need to learn how to listen to other points of view and disagree kindly	▸ I am usually polite and kind to teammates ▸ I usually listen to other points of view and disagree kindly	▸ I am polite and kind to teammates ▸ I listen to other points of view and disagree kindly	

COLLABORATION RUBRIC for PBL: *Team Performance*
(for grades 3-5)

	Below Standard	Approaching Standard	At Standard	Above Standard ✔
Makes and Follows Agreements	▸ We need to learn how to talk about how the team will work together ▸ We need to learn how to follow rules for collegial discussions, decision-making and conflict resolution ▸ We need to learn how to talk about how well agreements are being followed	▸ We try to talk about how the team will work together, but do not make agreements ▸ We usually follow rules for discussions, decision-making, and conflict resolution, but not always ▸ We sometimes talk about how well agreements are being followed but need help from the teacher to take appropriate steps when they are not	▸ We make agreements about how the team will work together ▸ We follow rules for discussions decision-making, and conflict resolution ▸ We honestly talk about how well agreements are being followed and take appropriate steps if they are not	
Organizes Work	▸ We get to work without creating a task list ▸ We need to learn how to set a schedule and track progress toward goals and deadlines ▸ We need to learn how to assign roles ▸ We need to learn how to use time and run meetings well, and organize our materials, drafts, notes	▸ We create a task list that divides project work among the team, but it may not be in detail or followed closely ▸ We set a schedule for doing tasks but do not follow it closely ▸ We assign roles but do not follow them, or we pick only one "leader" who makes most decisions ▸ We usually use time and run meetings well, but may occasionally waste time; we keep our materials, drafts, notes, but not always organized	▸ We create a detailed task list that divides project work fairly among the team ▸ We set a schedule and track progress toward goals and deadlines ▸ We assign roles based on team members' strengths ▸ We use time and runs meetings efficiently; we keep our materials, drafts, notes organized	
Works as a Whole Team	▸ We need to learn how to recognize or use special talents of team members ▸ We need to learn how to do the project as a team	▸ We try to use special talents of team members ▸ We do most project tasks separately and put them together at the end	▸ We recognize and use special talents of each team member ▸ We develop ideas and create products as a team; tasks done separately are brought to the team for feedback	

Teamwork Rubric for PBL
(for grades K-2)

I do my work for the team on time.

 1. still learning 2. sometimes  3. almost always

---

I help my team.

 1. still learning 2. sometimes  3. almost always

---

I listen to the ideas of my teammates.

 1. still learning 2. sometimes  3. almost always

---

I share my ideas with my team.

 1. still learning 2. sometimes  3. almost always

---

I treat my teammates with respect.

 1. still learning 2. sometimes   3. almost always

---

(Template for Letter to Parents)

Dear Parent or Guardian:

I am writing to tell you about an exciting project we are about to do in our class.

As you might know, in our school we use the teaching method of Project Based Learning, or PBL, to help students learn better. A project motivates students to gain knowledge, and they remember it longer. Projects give students the chance to apply the skills they learn in school to personally relevant and real-world situations. Your child also learns skills in PBL such as how to think critically, solve problems, work in teams, and make presentations. These skills will help students succeed in the future, both in school and in today's work world.

Our project is called [*name of project*] and it will last about [*duration*]. Students will learn about [*content, topics, standards information*]. The project's Driving Question, which focuses our work, is [*Driving Question*]. Students will be involved in [*researching on the Internet, interviewing community members, preparing an oral presentation, creating a video, etc.*]. Your child will work in a team, guided by me. We will be working with [*other teachers, schools, organizations, experts, etc.*]. We will be going outside the classroom to [*do field work at _____, meet with ___, etc.*].

At the end of the project students will make presentations to [*audience*]. This presentation will take place in [*location*] and is scheduled for [*date*] at [*time*]. We hope you will be able to attend.

Students will be assessed individually on their content knowledge, their collaboration skills, and their presentation skills. I have attached the rubrics we will use to guide the creation of [*product*] and assess students' work. You may find these helpful in understanding what we are asking students to do, and supporting your child during the project. As parents or guardians, you can discuss the project at home, encouraging your child to think hard and ask questions about the topic. You can also support the project by [*helping in the classroom, taking students on field work, providing expertise and resources, etc.*].

Please do not hesitate to contact me if you have any questions about the project!

Sincerely,

[*Name of Teacher*]

[*Contact Information*]

	PROJECT TEAM CONTRACT
Project Name:	
Team Members:	

Our Agreement

- We all promise to listen to each other's ideas with respect.

- We all promise to do our work as best as we can.

- We all promise to do our work on time.

- We all promise to ask for help if we need it.

- We all promise to _____

If someone on our team breaks one or more of our rules, the team may have a meeting and ask the person to follow our agreement. If the person still breaks the rules, we will ask our teacher to help find a solution.

Date: _____

Team Member Signatures:

_____   _____

_____   _____

_____   _____

Project Team Contract

We promise to:

_____

_____

_____

_____

_____

_____

_____

_____

_____

Date: _____

Team Member Signatures:

_____   _____

_____   _____

_____   _____

Project Team Work Plan

Project Name:	
Team Members:	

Product:		Due:	

What needs to be done?	Who will do this part?	By when?	✓ Done
			☐
			☐
			☐
			☐
			☐
			☐
			☐

Presentation Plan

What my presentation is about: _____

_____

_____

Who is my audience? _____

_____

_____

What do I want my audience to know, feel, or do? _____

_____

_____

How will I begin my presentation? _____

_____

_____

What will be in the middle part of my presentation? _____

_____

_____

_____

_____

How will I end my presentation? _____

_____

_____

What will I show or do to make my presentation interesting? _____

_____

_____

PRESENTATION DAY CHECKLIST

☐ Schedule of presentations set

☐ Guests/audience know when/where to attend

☐ Guest/audience materials duplicated

☐ Room arranged for presenters and audience

☐ Equipment/student materials in place

☐ Equipment tested (and tech support on stand-by)

☐ Teacher's materials in place

☐ Audience role explained

☐ Timekeeping device ready

PROJECT PRESENTATION AUDIENCE FEEDBACK

Student Team:

Project Name: **Date:**

Thank you for attending our project presentations and taking the time to write thoughtful answers to the following questions:

1. What did you learn from this presentation, or what did it make you think about?

2. What did you like about this presentation?

3. Do you have any questions about the topic or about how the project was done?

4. Any other comments about this presentation?

My Thoughts About the Project

Think about what you did in this project, and how well the project went.
Write your comments in the right column.

Student Name:	
Project Name:	
Driving Question:	
About Yourself:	
What is the most important thing you learned in this project:	
What do you wish you had spent more time on or done differently:	
What part of the project did you do your best work on:	
About the Project:	
What was the most enjoyable part of this project:	
What was the least enjoyable part of this project:	
How could your teacher(s) change this project to make it better next time:	

TEACHER'S POST-PROJECT REVIEW

| Project: | | Date | |

Project idea, design and implementation considerations	Reflections:
Student engagement	
Overall idea for the project	
Overall results for student learning	
Authenticity of project tasks and products	
Quality and use of Driving Question	
Scope: ▶ Length of time ▶ Complexity ▶ Number of subjects/people/organizations involved ▶ Use of technology	
Selection of content standards	

Selection of appropriate success skills	
Selection of culminating products and performances	
Effectiveness of Entry Event	
Quality of rubrics	
Quantity and mix of scaffolding and learning activities	
Ability of students to work well in groups	
Ability of students to work well independently	
Ability of students to use inquiry skills and think deeply	
My management of the process, coaching of students, and providing of support	
Involvement of other adults	
Adequacy of resources	

PROJECT DESIGN: OVERVIEW

Name of Project: Pizza and the World of Work	**Duration:** 10 weeks
Subject/Course: Social Studies, Science	**Teacher(s):** L. McConville
Other subject areas to be included, if any: English Language Arts, math, art	**Grade Level:** 2nd – 3rd

Key Knowledge and Understanding (CCSS or other standards)	**Social Studies:** (economics) buyers and sellers and examples of goods and services bought and sold in their community; specialization in jobs and businesses **Science:** plant structures and functions; energy and living things; compare and contrast solids, liquids, and gases based on the basic properties of each of these states of matter	**English Language Arts:** (reading) Identify, analyze, and apply knowledge of the purposes, structure, and elements of nonfiction or informational materials; (writing) write informative/explanatory texts to examine a topic and convey ideas and information clearly; take notes on sources **Math:** Develop understanding of fractions as numbers; Solve problems involving measurement and estimation of intervals of time, liquid volumes; Geometric measurement: understand concepts of area and relate area to multiplication and to addition

Success Skills (to be taught and assessed)	Critical Thinking/Problem Solving		Self-Management	X
	Collaboration		Other: Creativity and Innovation	X

Project Summary (include student role, issue, problem or challenge, action taken, and purpose/beneficiary)	Students study the world of work by talking with adults and running their own pizza business in the classroom. They read about work, interview their families and do field work in the community to find out how pizza shops are run. To prepare to operate a pizza restaurant for two days, the children write job descriptions, create advertisements, menus, and signs, rearrange and decorate their classroom, learn how to make pizza, and assemble ingredients. Students reflect on how it felt to perform different job duties, and on how much people are paid for doing various jobs. They learn how to calculate profit and decide how to spend it.
Driving Question	What does it mean to work?
Entry Event	The teacher engages students in a conversation about what kind of work they might want to do in the future, and describes the jobs she has held in the past (which includes working in pizza shops). She tells them she would like them to operate some sort of business in the classroom, and the children choose a pizza shop.
Products	**Individual:** (several individual writing assignments)	Specific content and competencies to be assessed: —ELA (writing) write informative/expository texts to examine a topic and convey ideas and information clearly; takes notes on sources
	Team: written job descriptions; plan for room arrangement; signs and advertisements; menu; perform all jobs during restaurant operation	Specific content and competencies to be assessed: —ELA (writing) write informative/expository texts to examine a topic and convey ideas and information clearly; takes notes on sources

PROJECT DESIGN: OVERVIEW

Making Products Public (include how the products will be made public and who students will engage with during/ at end of project)	Students will interview parents or family members and people who work in the community about their jobs. When they are setting up and running the pizza restaurant students will contact adults at school to take orders and explain the project to guests.
Resources Needed	On-site people, facilities: classroom; school students, teachers and staff (as customers)
	Equipment: classroom "kitchen" with food preparation areas, sink, toaster/convection ovens, cooking tools & cookware; card tables and chairs
	Materials: paper, paint for signs and menus; T-shirts & fabric paint for uniforms; clipboards for surveys; pizza ingredients; plates, cups, and utensils; tablecloths, napkins; dishwashing tubs, towels, soap and hot & cold water, fresh flowers, serving trays, aprons
	Community Resources: parents and community members; contacts in pizza restaurants

Reflection Methods (how individual, team, and/or whole class will reflect during/at end of project)	Journal/Learning Log	X	Focus Group
	Whole-Class Discussion	X	Fishbowl Discussion
	Survey		Other:

Notes:

PROJECT DESIGN: STUDENT LEARNING GUIDE

Project: Creatures in Oldham County

Driving Question: How can we make a picture book about the life cycle of creatures in Oldham County?

Final Product(s) Presentations, Performances, Products and/or Services	Learning Outcomes/Targets knowledge, understanding & success skills needed by students to successfully complete products	Checkpoints/Formative Assessments to check for learning and ensure students are on track	Instructional Strategies for All Learners provided by teacher, other staff, experts; includes scaffolds, materials, lessons aligned to learning outcomes and formative assessments
(individual **and** team) Written and illustrated book about animals in Oldham County	Difference between living vs. non-living things Life cycles in animals, stages of development	Human life cycle chart Teacher observation	Science Lesson—living vs. non-living things classification Construction of human life cycle chart with pictures and descriptions of each stage Video observations and discussions of life cycle of a chicken
	Animals in the woodlands in Oldham County Animals that can be observed on our campus	Research notebook check	Reader's workshop—Nonfiction reading about woodland animals Field experience—school grounds and woodlands
	How to generate research questions about the life cycle of an animal	Research notebook check	Researcher's workshop
	How to document observations about the life cycle of a fish, amphibian, or insect	Research notebook check	Researcher's workshop
	How to draw illustrations to document observations of the life cycle of a creature	Sketches/draft drawings of animal	Art lesson, with specialist
	How to add text to illustrations to explain the life cycle of a creature	Drafts of text for book	Writer's workshop
Oral presentation to representative of Oldham County Conservation District	Speaking skills Planning a simple presentation	Practice presentations to 4th/5th grades	Review presentation learning targets Observe and critique student presentations Practice summarizing and presenting

Project: Creatures in Oldham County (Kindergarten)   **Time Frame:** After Spring Break

MONDAY	TUESDAY	WEDNESDAY	THURSDAY	FRIDAY

PROJECT WEEK ONE

Notes: Bring butterfly larvae, ladybugs, and frog eggs into the classroom for observation this week

5 (Monday)
- Entry Event: guest speaker
- Need to Know activity
- Discuss Driving Question
- Explain major products, presentation and audience

Science workshop:
Living versus non-living things — classification
- Begin to create the concept word wall

Checkpoint: Review research questions and interview questions

6 (Tuesday)
Reader's workshop:
Determining importance and summarization — Nonfiction reading about woodland animals

Science workshop:
Human life cycles and how people change

7 (Wednesday)
Reader's workshop:
Determining importance and summarization — Nonfiction reading about woodland animals

Science workshop:
Animal life cycles — begin observing butterfly larvae, ladybugs, and frog eggs

8 (Thursday)
Reader's workshop:
Determining importance and summarization — Nonfiction reading about woodland animals

Science workshop:
Video — life cycle of a chicken

Math lesson:
begin keeping data on butterfly larvae, ladybugs, and frog eggs

9 (Friday)
Reader's workshop:
Determining importance and summarization — Nonfiction reading about woodland animals
- Form teams
- Group collaboration modeling
- Create project contracts

Science workshop and field experience:
Animals found in the woodlands in Oldham County — animals found near campus

PROJECT WEEK TWO

Notes: Call visiting expert mon. to discuss presentation

12 (Monday)
Reader's workshop:
Determining importance and summarization — Nonfiction reading about life cycles

Researcher's workshop:
Generating research questions about the life cycle of animals

Writer's workshop:
Generating "powerful" interview questions for visiting expert

Checkpoint: Review research questions and interview questions

13 (Tuesday)
Reader's workshop:
Determining importance and summarization — Nonfiction reading about life cycles

Researcher's workshop:
Documenting observations about life cycles of creatures
- Visit from expert from the community

14 (Wednesday)
Reader's workshop:
Determining importance and summarization — Nonfiction reading about life cycles

Researcher's workshop:
Documenting observations about life cycles of creatures

Checkpoint: Review documentations in research notebooks (meet with 1/3 of the class)

15 (Thursday)
Reader's workshop:
Determining importance and summarization — Nonfiction reading about life cycles

Researcher's workshop:
Documenting observations about life cycles of creatures

Checkpoint: Review documentations in research notebooks (meet with 1/3 of the class)

16 (Friday)
Reader's workshop:
Determining importance and summarization — Nonfiction reading about life cycles
- Continue observations and documentation in researcher's notebooks

Checkpoint: Review documentations in research notebooks (meet with remainder of the class)

Project: Creatures in Oldham County (Kindergarten)

MONDAY	TUESDAY	WEDNESDAY	THURSDAY	FRIDAY

PROJECT WEEK THREE

Notes: make sure paper & book cover material is ready by Thurs.

MONDAY	TUESDAY	WEDNESDAY	THURSDAY	FRIDAY
19 Reader's workshop: Determining importance and summarization— Nonfiction reading about life cycles – Continue observations and documentation in researcher's notebooks Writer's workshop: Creating narrative text illustrated book about life cycles	**20** Reader's workshop: Determining importance and summarization— Nonfiction reading about life cycles – Continue observations and documentation in researcher's notebooks Writer's workshop: Creating narrative text Art lesson from specialist: creating watercolor images of animal life cycles	**21** Reader's workshop: Determining importance and summarization— Nonfiction reading about life cycles – Continue observations and documentation in researcher's notebooks Writer's workshop: Creating narrative text Checkpoint: Critique drafts – work on watercolors	**22** Reader's workshop: Determining importance and summarization— Nonfiction reading about life cycles – Continue observations and documentation in researcher's notebooks Writer's workshop: Creating narrative text; polishing final draft Checkpoint: Critique drafts – work on watercolors	**23** Reader's workshop: Determining importance and summarization— Nonfiction reading about life cycles – Continue observations and documentation in researcher's notebooks Checkpoint: Text ready for book Checkpoint: watercolor illustrations done

PROJECT WEEK FOUR

Notes: call Conservation District mon. to discuss presentation details

MONDAY	TUESDAY	WEDNESDAY	THURSDAY	FRIDAY
26 – Begin assembling book Presentation workshop: Preparing for Presentations Checkpoint: Review plans for presentations with each team	**27** – Finish assembling book Presentations: morning meeting dress rehearsal	**28** Presentations: Practice in other grades classrooms	**29** Presentations to Oldham County Conservation District	**30** Celebration Project reflection: Revisiting the Driving Question— Journaling

4th Grade One-Year Curriculum Map with Projects

(Example from a school with partial integration of PBL and its literacy and numeracy programs. Projects take place during science and social studies time. Reading, writing, and speaking standards—and sometimes math—are reinforced through project work. Writing genres from standards are aligned to products required in various projects.)

Weeks	1-6 (Aug.-Sept.)	7-12 (Oct.-Nov.)	13-18 (Nov.-Dec.)	19-24 (Jan.-Feb.)	25-30 (Feb.-Mar.)	31-36 (Apr.-May)
Science Standards	**Physical Sciences:** Electricity and magnetism are related effects that have many useful applications in everyday life.	**Earth Sciences:** Waves, wind, water, and ice shape and reshape earth's land surface.	**Earth Sciences:** The properties of rocks and minerals reflect the processes that formed them.		**Life Sciences:** All organisms need energy and matter to live and grow. Living organisms depend on one another and on their environment for survival.	
Project	Students use knowledge of conductors and insulation to design a safe electronic toy. **Major Products:** Electronic toy, research notebook, and presentation	Students create digital stories to illustrate how various land features of California were formed, e.g., Yosemite, beaches, sand dunes, Central Valley, etc. **Major Products:** Digital story, research notebook, and presentation	Students solve a problem in a scenario involving an investor who wants advice on investing money in the mining business in California, given its mining history, geologic diversity, and mineral wealth. **Major Products:** Research notebook, written report with annotated map, and oral presentation of solution to the problem. **Integrated English Language Arts Standards:** Write informative/explanatory texts to examine a topic and convey ideas and information clearly. **Writing Workshops in Project:** Research Report: finding and evaluating information; topic sentences and supporting facts		Students create videos to show how various animals in their region are dependent on ecosystems. **Major Products:** Narrated video, research notebook, and presentation	

continued

Weeks	1-6 (Aug.-Sept.)	7-12 (Oct.-Nov.)	13-18 (Nov.-Dec.)	19-24 (Jan.-Feb.)	25-30 (Feb.-Mar.)	31-36 (Apr.-May)
Social Studies Standards	**State History:** Students describe the social, political, cultural, and economic life and interactions among people of California from the pre-Columbian societies to the Spanish mission and mexican rancho periods.		**State History:** Students explain the economic, social, and political life in California from the establishment of the Bear Flag Republic through the mexican–American war, the Gold Rush, and the granting of statehood.	**State History:** Students explain how California became an agricultural and industrial power, tracing the transformation of the California economy and its political and cultural development since the 1850s.	**Geography:** Students demonstrate an understanding of the physical and human geographic features that define places and regions in California.	
Project	Students study paintings, artifacts, myths & legends, and historical evidence to explore what life was like for Native Americans and how it changed with the arrival of the Spanish. **Major Products:** Written stories/historical narratives about a Native American before and after the arrival of the Spanish, presented in a dramatic reading or podcast. **Integrated English Language Arts Standards:** Write narratives to develop real or imagined experiences or events using effective technique, descriptive details, and clear event sequences. **Writing Workshops in Project:** Historical Narrative: writing a good beginning; keeping to the focus; varying sentences. Descriptive writing: ordering information; using sensory language; sentence combining		Students write and produce a play that captures the experience of miners and various ethnic groups during the Gold Rush period, with references to historical events. **Major Products:** written script and performance of the play. **Writing Workshops in Project:** Developing plot, character, and setting; writing dialogue; using possessives	Students create web pages that explain how California became an agricultural and industrial power. **Major Products:** Web pages on different time periods and developments, with text, timeline, and images	Students develop their answer to the question, "what is most special or unique about the geography of The Golden State?" **Major Product:** Opinion piece for state government web page to attract tourists. **Integrated English Language Arts Standards:** Write opinion pieces on topics or texts, supporting a point of view with reasons and information. **Writing Workshops in Project:** Opinion Piece: main idea and details; introductions and conclusions; pronoun reference	

SPOTLIGHT PROJECTS

We've chosen seven projects to provide you with an idea of what it's like to design and implement PBL. These projects are from different teachers and schools and illustrate the various forms PBL can take. We discussed some of the details of these projects in the chapters of this book. In the summary at the beginning of each project you'll find information about how to find it online or contact the project author if you want to learn more about it.

- **Kindergarten Science, Language Arts, Art:
  "Creatures in Oldham County"**

  This project takes place in a rural school in Kentucky and is a good example of a project in which children create an authentic product — an illustrated book about local animals, to be displayed at a local government office.

- **1st Grade Social Studies, Language Arts:
  "Cool with School Rules"**

  This is an example of a project in which students investigate and solve a real-world problem: deciding what rules should govern behavior in their school playground, lunchroom, and other areas, and making other students aware of these rules.

- **2nd-3rd Grade Social Studies, Language Arts, Math:**
  "Pizza Shops and the World of Work"

  A project from an urban school in Boston in which students create an event—running a pizza restaurant out of their classroom—with the added dimension of thinking critically about what it means to work.

- **3rd Grade Social Studies, Language Arts:**
  "Parkland on Display"

  This is an example of the popular "museum exhibit" type of project that presents information to the community. From a school in urban Louisville, Kentucky, this multifaceted project is carried out by all four third grade classrooms working together.

- **4th Grade Science, Social Studies, Language Arts:**
  "The Shrimp Project"

  This is an example of an ambitious, lengthy project that was not designed in advance by the teacher, but which sprang from the students' real desire to do something about an environmental issue they learned about.

- **5th Grade Math:**
  "Selling a Cell"

  A "classic" math project used to teach algebra and pre-algebra concepts and skills, in which students decide which cell phone plan best fits their family's needs.

- **5th Grade Science:**
  "What's With This Guy?"

  In this project students investigate and propose possible solutions for an authentic problem, in a fictitious scenario in which they play the role of medical school students.

Project #1: Creatures in Oldham County

THE PROJECT IN BRIEF

Project Title: Creatures in Oldham County

Project Author: Abbey Flynn, St. Francis School, Goshen, Kentucky

Content Area: Science, with Language Arts, Math, and Art

Grade Level: Kindergarten

Duration: 3 weeks; approximately 1½ hours per day, 5 days a week

Driving Question: How can we create a picture book about the life cycles of creatures in Oldham County?

Project Summary: Students are asked to create an illustrated book about the life cycles of local wild animals, to be displayed at the office of the Oldham County Conservation District. Working in teams, students generate research questions, read about and document their observations of animals in local woodlands, and follow the life cycles of amphibians and insects raised in the classroom. Finally, they paint watercolor pictures and write text about one animal selected by the team, and present their work to representatives of the County Conservation District.

Major Student Products: Illustrated book about life cycles of local animals; oral presentation; research notebook including questions, observations & sketches, photographs taken during field experiences, and interview questions for experts.

For More Information: Contact Abbey Flynn via her school's website at **www.stfrancisschool.org**

How the Project Was Conceived and Planned

Abbey Flynn developed her idea for a project by reviewing her science curriculum map and thinking about her students' interests. She and her students are fascinated by animals and love the outdoors, and their independent school is located in a semi-rural farming community next to a nature preserve with abundant wild life. Abbey wanted to plan a project that capitalized on this location.

Driving Question: How can we create a picture book about the life cycles of creatures in Oldham County?

As a teacher, Abbey strives to go beyond fact-focused instruction, favoring in-depth exploration of rich content despite the young age of her students. She identified in her science content standards some critical understandings that she wanted her students to be able to generalize and apply to subsequent studies: "Animals go through a series of orderly changes. Changes in living things occur in cycles. Life cycles differ among the various animals." Abbey wanted students to learn about these concepts in a local, interesting context, so her project focused on inquiry into the life cycles of animals that live in their county. An illustrated book seemed like a natural way for her kindergarteners to showcase what they learned. To heighten the sense of authenticity and help motivate students to do high-quality work, she asked a local conservation organization, the Oldham County Conservation District, to get involved. Abbey decided to launch the project by having a representative from the Conservation District deliver a memo to the students requesting them to create a book for display at the District office, and to make a presentation to the District's staff.

How the Project Was Managed

After launching the project, Abbey provided each student with a "research notebook" in which they would record questions they wanted or needed to answer, keep notes and drawings, and keep track of their progress through the project. She introduced the idea of a life cycle by guiding students through a reflection about the human life cycle and the ways in which people change. Students created human life cycle charts that contained pictures and descriptions of each stage. Abbey also facilitated a series of experiences to spark student curiosity and build additional background knowledge about the topic. She brought butterfly larvae, ladybugs, and frog eggs into the classroom for observation. The children were introduced to the life cycle of a chicken through video clips. They went outside to observe animals found in the woodlands near the school campus. Throughout these experiences, the children generated research questions such as "Does the animal's life cycle start in an egg?" and "Does the animal change shape as it gets older?" and "Does the animal live in different places as it gets older?" which would later guide them in creating the illustrated book for the County Conservation District.

Divided into teams, students chose an animal in the woodlands to focus on. They used their research notebooks to record more research questions about its life cycle, and recorded information to help answer their questions. Abbey continued to build background knowledge through fiction and non-fiction in reader's workshops, using books such as *The Very Hungry Caterpillar* and *From Tadpole to Frog*. She led literature circles to facilitate the inquiry process by reading with each team and guiding students to discuss their learning and generate additional research questions. (See the **Teaching and Learning Guide** and **Project Calendar** on pages 148-150 for more detail on what took place on each day of the project.) To help her teach the science content knowledge, Abbey used the Smart Board with students on several occasions to put animals in life cycle circles, categorize different life cycles, and do other visually-oriented activities about animals around the school. Math lessons were worked into the project as the children tracked the number of days it took for the butterfly larvae, ladybugs, and frogs to go through the various stages in their life cycles.

Every day as they worked, Abbey assessed the students' science content knowledge informally. By circulating around the room observing their discussions, journal entries, and interest levels, and stopping at each team multiple times to ask questions, she could gauge if they were on the right track. She also collected the research notebooks each day to look at them and write some guiding questions to prompt students' thinking for the following day. During whole-group discussions, Abbey asked questions and listened to the children explain what they were observing. They also completed several tasks that required each child individually to label or order life cycles, which were collected and assessed.

When the students were ready to create the illustrated book, Abbey used a writer's workshop approach to guide them through the process of developing narrative text. The school's art teacher came in on two days to help the children create water color images of the animal life cycles to go with their writing. The class prepared for their presentations by discussing the qualities of an effective presentation, critiquing video clips of student presentations, and engaging in a dress rehearsal by presenting to 4th and 5th grade classes in school. The students were so eager to share their knowledge that they couldn't restrain themselves from occasionally getting into someone else's part of the presentation or talking over each other. After a little corrective feedback, the children spoke clearly and took turns when the time came for the final presentation to the representative from the County Conservation District. Abbey noted with pride, "The representative was so impressed with not only their work, vocabulary, and knowledge, but their enthusiasm for science. I loved it when she was asking them questions to stump them and they knew every answer!"

Reflecting on the Project

Abbey was struck by how her students became stronger readers, writers, scientists, mathematicians—and better classmates—just from a simple project. Many of the skills they learned in this one project would have taken longer to teach, Abbey estimates, if she had broken them apart and taught each one separately. Teaching students how to write sentences, for example, would have taken weeks, if not months. Instead, the children were eager to use their observation journals and wanted to know how to write exactly what they were witnessing. She took this opportunity to demonstrate writing a complete thought and how writers use periods to mark the end of that thought. They were then able to naturally write complete sentences that included nouns, verbs, and even adjectives.

The children felt a sense of ownership over their learning. Abbey noted that they were completely engaged in tasks that had previously bored them. Science journals became thrilling and students were eager to fill up all of the pages, and walking on trails outside became purposeful instead of a "free for all." Reading non-fiction texts suddenly became a task of locating important information instead of just listening. Working with partners became time to become experts instead of time to argue. Observing became quiet time to watch and use their senses instead of create mischief, and "best of all, sharing time became a time to teach the teacher."

Abbey remembers a powerful moment in the project:

"When I asked each team to tell me what they wanted to write to go with the illustrations of the animals, I was prepared to write a sentence or two on the board, and was blown away when the words started spilling from their mouths. They wanted to share so much that I had a difficult time keeping up with their words. They were on the edges of their seats, working together to add and comment on what the others had said. I was most impressed by their use of scientific vocabulary. This for me was one of those moments when I knew that I had reached my class."

Project #2: Cool with School Rules

THE PROJECT IN BRIEF

Project Title: Cool with School Rules

Project Author: Dana Holstein, Brookview Elementary School, Foster, West Virginia

Content Area: Social Studies, with Language Arts

Grade Level: 1st

Duration: 3 weeks; approximately 1 hour per day, 4-5 days a week

Driving Question: What rules and consequences should we have at our school?

Project Summary: Students work in teams to propose rules for different areas in the school, as part of an effort to enhance the school culture and create a revised discipline plan. Each team selects an area to develop rules for: the classrooms, bathrooms, hallways, cafeteria, or the playground. Students generate questions, review sample discipline plans from other schools, and interview students, teachers, and school administrators to get their views on how school rules should be structured. To culminate the project, each student creates a poster and each team makes a video commercial to persuade the school to adopt their proposed rules.

Major Student Products: List of rules for selected area; video commercials presented to an audience; illustrated poster.

For More Information: This project may be found in the West Virginia Department of Education project library at **wvde.state.wv.us/teach21/pbl.html**.

How the Project Was Conceived and Planned

Dana's school was undergoing many changes at the time when she began planning what and how to teach for the year. One of the ways the staff was hoping to improve the school was to create a new discipline plan that specified rules and consequences for behavior in various places on campus. Learning about the role rules play in society was an important objective in the first grade social studies curriculum, so Dana decided a project that helped the school accomplish its goals would be a great way to bring in a real world problem for the students to solve. She knew the children would find the topic relevant, and that they would enjoy using technology to create videos and posters. They would have plenty of opportunities to build their English/Language Art skills in reading, writing, listening and speaking as well as learn to work together in teams.

Driving Question: What rules and consequences should we have at our school?

How the Project Was Managed

To launch the project, Dana invited the school principal into her classroom to ask her students for help. The principal told them he was concerned about students' safety and proper behavior in several places around the school, including the lunchroom, the playground, and the hallways. He asked them to decide some rules for each area, and to create posters and videos to tell other students about the rules. He also asked the students to send him a list of suggested consequences for breaking a rule, to help him and the staff decide what they should be. Dana followed this Entry Event with a discussion about "bad behavior" the students had seen around the school, and started making a list. They talked about which behaviors created safety problems vs. which created problems between children, such as hurt feelings or unfairness. This got the class thinking about how the consequences for breaking rules might vary.

To build students' knowledge about the topic, and to help address her social studies standards, Dana had a local police officer visit the class to discuss the importance of rules, the difference between rules and laws, and how laws and rules are enforced. Dana captured the officer's comments, terms used, and responses to student questions on a chart to display in the room during the project. She continued to build students' knowledge by showing examples of rules and discipline plans from other schools, which the class read. Students generated questions and then interviewed teachers and a principal from another local school by phone about their experiences in creating and enforcing fair rules and consequences in response to problems in their school.

Students were divided into teams of four, chosen by Dana. Each team drew a piece of paper from a basket with the area of the school for which they would generate rules. Dana discussed and modeled the expectations for teamwork skills and met with each team to develop group contracts. The teams began deciding 3-5 rules for their specific area of the school. For example, one of the rules for the bathroom was, "Don't splash water," which the students said created a safety problem from slipping, as well as wasted water. One of the most important aspects of managing the project were the daily "exit slips" turned in by each team to report on their progress, which provided Dana with useful feedback about "what you did today/ what you need" so she could address any problems that were arising. She met with each team at different times during the project to discuss their progress.

The principal stopped by regularly to hear the teams' ideas for rules and give them feedback. Each team decided how they would advertise their rule, wrote scripts and storyboards, and rehearsed their scenes and voiceovers. Once they were ready, the children used flip cameras to create 2-5 minute video commercials to advertise their rules. Individually, students used laptops to create posters (using glogster. com's online poster-designing tool) displaying the rules for their area.

To conclude the project, the class invited the principal, the school's parent-teacher organization, police officers, and other community members to engage in a poster gallery walk and critique the commercial presentations. As guests walked through the gallery, they used sticky notes to make comments about the posters. Each team showed their video commercials and explained to the community members what it means to be responsible and why rules are important.

Reflecting on the Project

Dana found the project to be an engaging, interactive way to teach important social studies curriculum standards, giving students the opportunity to understand the importance of rules in school and the real world. The project taught lessons about what a community was—and how research could be conducted—by providing opportunities to talk to community members, teachers, and people from other schools. The children learned new skills in using technology, taking pride in how they were able to use flip cameras to produce videos and the Glogster website to design and print posters. The project gave these first graders a glimpse of what it means to think critically as they discussed the differences among other school discipline plans. The discipline plans also gave students

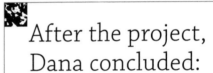

After the project, Dana concluded:

"Students were very excited about this project. They were engaged and felt a sense of ownership, taking pride in creating rules for their school. Before it started I was afraid I would not be able to reach first graders and that they were too young to complete such a project, but they were able to do it and loved it."

an opportunity to learn to read a new form of text. Working in teams allowed the children to practice important success skills: how to plan tasks, meet their responsibilities, and help each other create a high-quality product. Finally, even for these very young students, the project taught them they could make a valuable contribution to their community: their school.

Project #3: Pizza Shops and the World of Work

THE PROJECT IN BRIEF

Project Title: Pizza Shops and the World of Work

Project Author: Laurel McConville, Mission Hill School, Boston MA

Content Area: Social Studies, with Language Arts and Math

Grade Level: 2nd and 3rd

Duration: 10 weeks; 1-2 hours a day, 4-5 days per week

Driving Question: What does it mean to work?

Project Summary: Students organize, create and run a pizza shop for two days inside their classroom. Leading up to this event is an in-depth study of work. The children interview people at home about their jobs and venture into the community to talk with workers and learn about the pizza restaurant business. Working in committees, students conduct customer surveys, develop menus, design uniforms, create work schedules and job descriptions, advertise their business, and schedule reservations. In the pizza shop the children take turns doing different jobs — reflecting on which ones seem more "fair" than others — as they make pizza from scratch for both delivery and dine-in service.

Major Student Products: Journals with research notes and reflective writing; work schedules and job descriptions; restaurant signs, menus, uniforms, advertisements; homemade pizza.

For More Information: Contact Laurel McConville at the Mission Hill School in Boston, MA at **laurel.missionhill@ gmail.com.**

How the Project was Conceived and Planned

At Mission Hill School, located in urban Boston, the whole school studies three thematic units a year. In this particular year, when they were to begin the "World of Work" theme, 2nd-3rd grade teacher Laurel McConville wanted to provide children with the real experience of working. She went home one night, after a lively discussion with colleagues about the upcoming theme, and thought about her own work experiences. She had worked in two different pizza shops throughout high school and in college, so it was a business she knew inside and out. She decided on a project: the class would create an authentic pizza shop, so the children could feel the real work behind something that they were familiar with and likely took for granted.

Driving Question: What does it mean to work?

Laurel wanted her 7-9 year olds to experience the thought and labor that goes into providing people with food — and to come to the realization that some of the hardest, most labor intensive jobs pay the least amount of money, since one of her goals was to have students think critically about equity as it relates to work. She also knew that this experience would be rich in math, science and art. Students could practice addition, subtraction, multiplication and division as they learned about money, profit, sales, and making change. Other real-world applications of math would present themselves when scheduling work assignments and when cooking, which involved fractions, measurements and temperatures. The children would learn science through the study of yeast and where ingredients come from, and how they are processed. For example, they would learn about plant structure (some spices are seeds, some are leaves!), variety (mushrooms are fungus! wheat is a grass!), and growth (yeast makes carbon dioxide bubbles in bread!). Art and graphic design skills would come into play when the children made menus, signs, and advertisements for their restaurant.

How the Project was Managed

To launch the project, Laurel started a conversation with her students about what they thought they wanted to do for work as adults. The class began thinking about what it means to work. The children made small books called "People I Know and the Work They Do," interviewed adults at home about their work, and wrote about what they heard. Laurel created a timeline of the work she had done in her life so far, a long rolled-up paper that they unrolled together as a class and took a look at. The children were interested in several of the jobs she'd had, but working in pizza restaurants elicited quite a bit of excitement, which she'd expected. Laurel then told the class she was hoping they could create a business in their classroom and was wondering what kind of business they might like to have. Almost all of the class wanted to start – guess what– a pizza business. She said she knew a lot about that kind of work and would be happy to help.

The next stage of the project involved dramatic play. Laurel knew that nine weeks of planning for a restaurant's "grand opening" was not going to be very satisfying for seven, eight and nine year olds who felt ready to make and sell pizza upon hearing the idea. She knew they needed some time to act out their visions and understandings of work as they knew it; to play out the roles and negotiations they see in adult settings; and to feel that the work was theirs to tackle. She and the children collected aprons, rolling pins, trays, pizza boxes, order pads, and a small cash register, among other authentic tools, and made lots of dough. It was an exciting time. The classroom transformed into a pretend restaurant. The children turned the coatroom into the kitchen, complete with spatulas and a stove. They wore aprons and took orders from each other. They served play dough pizzas and cylinder blocks became straws in the beverages on their trays. The room was bustling with imaginative visions of a real restaurant. Each day, the language, roles and authenticity grew as new ideas from the real world were being incorporated and exchanged.

During this stage, four children at a time worked in the small kitchen area with Laurel or her student teacher to practice making real pizza—measuring ingredients, reading recipes, setting the oven temperature and timer, and making scientific observations. The class created a calendar for recording when adults in the building requested deliveries. They decided to try out their pizza-making skill by delivering two personal pizzas a day around lunchtime, taking orders the day before. After a delivery, students delivered a receipt and comment card, to get feedback on their work. The class saved copies of receipts to keep track of the money they made, and read the comment cards at class meetings and hung them in their kitchen.

The class also did research during this time, taking trips out into the community to visit a variety of pizza shops and ask the workers questions. Restaurant employees visited the classroom to talk about the work that they do and answer questions. One expert guest came in and taught the children how to properly stretch and toss dough.

Laurel incorporated reading, writing, and math lessons by tying almost everything to the Driving Question and pizza. She read aloud every day for 30 minutes, selecting stories about work and pizza making. For example, they read *The Little Red Hen (Makes a Pizza)* and Richard Scarry's *What Do People Do All Day?* The students also read takeout menus from around the neighborhood and pizza places around the city, kept in a bin labeled "menus" in the classroom library. All the children, even reluctant readers, were drawn to them regularly, comparing prices and reading menu items and ingredient lists, information about ordering and the restaurant's hours and location. They often copied or recreated the menus whenever they had the chance, before they began to write their own. And of course, as the time to make their own pizza got closer, the students read and discussed many recipes.

After four weeks the children were ready to begin planning and creating their restaurant. The class decided to form six committees with the following tasks:

- **Architecture and Design:** Draw a map of what the classroom would look like and plan for what furniture had to be moved, what structures would be built out of blocks, what materials were needed, where the kitchen, tables, and cash register would be, and so on.

- **Uniforms:** Design various logos and agree on one. Draw pictures of what each worker would need to wear (different types of aprons, hats, etc) and use fabric paint to make a shirt for each employee.

- **Job Descriptions and Scheduling:** Choose the jobs they would need and write a job description with an illustration for each one. Create a schedule for the workers for the two days the restaurant would be open. (Each worker was to have at least one turn at each of the jobs, and also have one shift off.)

- **Menu and Surveys:** Walk around the school surveying people to find out what they like on pizza. Create a tally chart of favorite toppings and use the results to create a menu and the specialty pizzas they would offer.

- **Restaurant Banner:** Draw a picture of what their eight-foot banner would look like, and then measure, cut, and paint it. (The restaurant name was painted in the middle and surrounded with pictures of food and interestingly, dollar bills).

- **Advertising:** Decide how and when to advertise. (They made posters to hang around the school, drew a small advertisement for the school newsletter, and made announcements at the weekly All School Share.)

During the next few weeks, children met with their committees to plan and carry out the work. Each committee had a folder to keep their work and plans in, as well as notes, guiding questions and organizational materials that Laurel provided.

The students continued making deliveries to the adults around the building. They kept a lot of data and talked about the math involved in their work along the way (How many pizzas were we able to make from one bag of flour? How many pizzas did a pound of mozzarella cover?). They asked each family to "loan" them one bag of flour, one packet of yeast, one jar of sauce, and one block of mozzarella cheese, and to provide a receipt so they could be paid back later on. This began discussions about sales and profit. They also brainstormed a list of restaurant names, debated which was most fitting and voted for "One Bite of Heaven."

The final stage was the grand opening. The intensely focused last-minute activity included preparing and decorating the room, assembling ingredients, and scheduling reservations for other classes, adults in the building, and families. When the big day came, the children took their places at the various stations around the restaurant and performed their duties well. When workers had a shift off they used the time to reflect in their work journal, using pictures and words, on their experiences performing different jobs. Over the course of the two days, the class served pizza to almost two hundred people. Drinks were spilled and orders got backed up from time to time, and the workers were exhausted, but they were thrilled.

Reflecting on the Project

After the restaurant closed its doors — and *almost* everything was cleaned up and put away — Laurel and the children returned to the Driving Question and reflected on, "What does it mean to work?"

The class talked about how it felt to work so hard, and which jobs felt better to do than others. Many of the children liked being the manager. Many did not like being the dishwasher. They talked about which jobs they found more stimulating and which ones were the hardest. Laurel turned the discussion toward the topic of wages and the fact that some of the hardest, most labor-intensive jobs pay workers the least amount of money, in this country and around the world. Some children had heard about child labor and unlivable wages in other parts of the world and brought that into the conversation. The children talked about fairness in the world of work, and what they thought was fair in terms of duties, time, and wages. To conclude the discussion of work, Laurel asked students to write some reflective, concluding sentences in their journals.

Laurel commented on the importance of the project:

"It is a memory that the children hold dear. In their fifth grade Recollections speeches nearly every one of them mentioned the experience as one of the most memorable times of their elementary years. Real learning is so important. School is a place where children of all ages should be getting their hands and clothes dirty every day. They should leave with stimulated minds, asking more questions than they came in with."

After the class counted the money they received, and paid back what they owed their suppliers, they found they had a bit less than half left as profit. They discussed what to do with it, and after considering limousine rides and big purchases for the classroom, they eventually decided to donate the money to poverty relief in Zimbabwe (after they had watched a video about its struggles) and Haiti (where many members of their school community were from).

Looking back on the project, Laurel reflected on some things she might do differently next time. The quality of student work was one area that needed improvement. "In hindsight, this project did not include enough drafts of committee work, or perhaps enough critical feedback. I left a lot open-ended for the children to decide as opposed to breaking things down sequentially for them to tackle one piece at a time. I think that for the group of children that I had at the time, the latter approach would have helped to create higher quality products in the end." She also points out the need for checkpoints. "I run project time differently now than I did then. Each child must complete certain tasks each week during project time to move forward on a project, but they have the choice of when to complete it within the week. We use checklists to keep track. I find that running project time this way increases overall investment and productivity. I remember some fruitless committee work times during the pizza shop project!"

Project #4: Parkland on Display

Project Title: Parkland on Display

Project Author: Carolyn Connor and Jamey Herdelin, with Amy Brown, Sarah Herberger, Sheila Rivers, Patty Voss, and Kai Walz, Maupin Elementary School, Jefferson County Public School, Louisville, KY

Content Area: Social Studies, Language Arts, and Math

Grade Level: 3rd

Duration: 8 weeks; approximately 1 hour per day, 5 days a week

Driving Question: How can we preserve and share the historical and cultural wealth of the Parkland Community?

Project Summary: In this grade-level-wide project, students learn about the people, places, and events that shaped the development of the Parkland community in urban Louisville, Kentucky. Each 3rd grade classroom focuses on one aspect of the local neighborhood and student teams conduct research using primary source information, community speakers, and field experiences. Students share their knowledge by creating multi-faceted museum-like displays, culminating with a showcase for the community. Students also publish and distribute a newsletter to the school, parents, and neighborhood residents, to help them develop and preserve their own sense of the history and cultural wealth of the community. In the final step of the project the entire 3rd grade plans and paints a mural that depicts their hopeful vision of Parkland in the future.

Major Student Products: Museum exhibit and showcase; community newsletter; mural

For More Information: Contact Carolyn Connor at the Maupin School at **carolyn.connor@jefferson.kyschools.us**

How the Project was Conceived and Planned:

In the spring of 2010 the Maupin School, located in a low-income, high-minority population area of Louisville began to develop innovative ways, including PBL, to incorporate core content with success skills. The 3rd grade teaching team, which included the school's PBL specialist, library media specialist, and technology teacher, reviewed their school's social studies test scores, which were lower than they wanted to them to be. They decided that making the study of history more relevant to students might engage them in learning and help them retain their knowledge even long after the test was done. This led them to design a grade-level-wide project over the summer, one that would challenge students to learn about the history of their neighborhood and share their findings with others. The team hoped that students would take ownership of the project and join with everyone in the community to take pride in who they are and where they come from. Their ambitious project had three major components: a museum exhibit and showcase for the community, a newsletter distributed to the school and community, and a mural expressing hopes for Parkland's future.

> Driving Question: How can we preserve and share the historical and cultural wealth of the Parkland Community?

The content standards for 3rd grade social studies, which included local history, the use of primary sources, and map-reading skills, were a natural fit with the project. The team incorporated literacy goals by targeting non-fiction reading skills as well as writing. One of the writing requirements in the 3rd grade English Language Arts standards is the feature article, which included the skills of interviewing, taking notes, summarizing, editing and revision. Math skills could be reinforced when students collected data on local businesses and created line and bar graphs to represent it. The teaching team also recognized the importance of developing students' critical thinking skills and their ability to use technology, with support from the technology teacher and library media specialist.

How the Project was Managed

The team launched the project with an event called the "Neighborhood Walk." Following a short slide presentation, students were challenged to locate a variety of historic locations during their walk. They were accompanied by their representative in the state legislature, who was a native of Parkland. He became a primary source of information, sharing his knowledge and love of the community while answering questions posed by students. Upon returning to the library that same day, the students were presented with the Driving Question and goals for the project. Back in their classrooms, the teachers bego to build background knowledge for the inquiry process by distributing a variety of text materials in a packet containing primary source documents, articles, maps and photographs. These materials were used to teach reading skills throughout the project.

The next activity was a field experience involving a famous resident of the neighborhood, champion boxer Muhammad Ali. The students visited the Muhammad Ali Center, where they learned about his childhood in the neighborhood and contributions to the world beyond the streets of their city. Students learned to use a variety of ways of gathering information — writing notes, taking photos, drawing, and videotaping — and were asked to think critically and reflect on what they saw and felt. This experience also gave students some insight into how to create engaging museum displays, which was a critical component of the project.

After this experience, the four classroom teachers explained to their classes what their specific focus would be: people, places, commercial development, or events that shaped and changed the Parkland community. They organized students into teams, and led them in generating a list of questions to investigate. This was a critical step for developing ideas for a feature article in the newsletter they needed to write, as well as developing the focus for their museum exhibits and culminating showcase. The 3rd graders divided the tasks among their team and began to research in earnest. Time was allotted each afternoon for project work, since the mornings were protected time for the school's literacy and math programs.

Several other products were required in the project in addition to the newsletter article, museum exhibit, and mural:

- Students in the classroom that focused on *people* wrote and presented biographical sketches of famous residents, such as Muhammad Ali, Milburn T. Maupin, and Lymon T. Johnson.

- Students in the classroom that focused on *places* created a brochure for a walking tour of the neighborhood, photo exhibits, and replicas and drawings of famous architectural structures.

- Students in the classroom that focused on *events* created a timeline, using Comic Life and PhotoStory 3, showing highlights of significant events that reshaped the neighborhood.

- Students in the classroom that focused on *commercial development* created, conducted, and graphed the results of a survey about businesses that exist and that residents would like to see. The students also mapped the commercial district and made videos highlighting their interviews with current business owners.

The museum exhibit showcase in the library media center was a big success. Students delivered polished presentations to parents and community guests as they stood before their displays. Working with the art specialist, the 3rd graders culminated the project by creating a colorful mural on the wall of the library media center, reflecting their pride in and hopes for their community.

Reflecting on the Project

The project became quite important for the school and its community. The students' sense of pride in their community grew as they met people and formed connections to their neighborhood. The school district's newsletter highlighted the project. The teaching team was pleased to see how much the project was valued by parents, especially those who grew up in Parkland. They called to volunteer to help and contributed stories for the newsletter, which they found informative. One reader commented, "I've lived here all my life & never knew what that plaque meant!" Some students at the school came from other neighborhoods where people had a negative image of Parkland, and the project changed their views. "I never knew so many wonderful things happened here," said a boy from a suburban home in his written reflections on the project. The project brought the teaching team together, too, sparking a lot of enthusiasm and creative teaching ideas.

In terms of meeting their goals for student learning, the teachers found positive results in their assessment of the students' knowledge of history facts and concepts. Reading and writing skills definitely improved, and the students knew how to use a variety of sources and tools for research. And there was plenty of evidence that students could think critically, work in teams, make presentations, and use technology. The school's librarian even noticed a welcome side effect of the project: more students were checking out biographies in general, not just those needed for the project.

The teaching team noticed a special effect on some students:

"The project was especially beneficial for struggling students. It gave them something to connect to, a sense of ownership of their learning. One particular child who is extremely challenging — to see him so focused was amazing. He came up with history facts for a song they wrote and really kept his team on task."

Project #5: The Shrimp Project

THE PROJECT IN BRIEF

Project Title: The Shrimp Project

Project Author: Laurette Rogers, formerly at Brookside School, San Anselmo, CA

Content Area: Science, with integrated English/Language Arts, Social Studies

Grade Level: 4th

Duration: 6 months; 2-4 hours per week

Driving Question: What can we do to save endangered species?

Project Summary: Students plan and conduct a campaign to save an endangered species, the California freshwater shrimp, and engage in field work in a local watershed to restore riparian corridors that provide habitat for the shrimp and other species. Students do research, create public awareness-raising materials, conduct a fundraising campaign, write letters and make presentations to the community and to government officials. Field activities include planting trees, shrubs, and grasses, preventing soil erosion, and wildlife observation.

Major Student Products: Oral presentations; video public service announcements; t-shirts; various written products including research reports, letters, press releases, and a newsletter.

For More Information: Contact Laurette Rogers at Students and Teachers Restoring a Watershed (STRAW) at lrogers@prbo.org.

How the Project Was Conceived and Planned

(Note: This ambitious project originated in 1992 and since then it has evolved and spread to other schools. We will describe its first year. Teacher Laurette Rogers now directs the STRAW Project — Students and Teachers Restoring a Watershed — which coordinates a network of teachers, students, restoration specialists and other community members as they plan and implement watershed studies and restoration projects in the San Francisco Bay Area.)

The project began in November when 4th grade teacher Laurette Rogers showed her class a video about endangered species around the world, which was the Entry Event for the project. Noticing the students seemed depressed afterward, she conducted a discussion during which one boy raised his hand to ask, "What can we do to save endangered species?" The question launched Laurette and her class into an inquiry to determine the possibilities for taking action. They brainstormed a list of possibilities, and decided that simply writing letters about the issue, raising money for environmental groups, or creating a general public awareness campaign in their school and community would not be satisfying enough — they wanted to actually help save a species directly.

Driving Question:
What can we do to save endangered species?

By contacting the California State Adopt-a-Species Program, Laurette found out that three endangered animal species lived in their region: a salmon, a trout, and a shrimp. The winner by a vote of the students was the California freshwater shrimp, whose habitat in local creeks was being lost due to development and agriculture. Laurette could see that through this project she would not only be able to teach her science curriculum and social studies concepts, but would also have an authentic purpose for students to build reading, writing, and math skills. So began what would become a life-changing event for Laurette and her class.

How the Project Was Managed

Students worked in teams to learn all they could, from the natural history of the shrimp to the agencies responsible for their welfare and the laws affecting them. As part of their investigation, students read various informational materials, interviewed experts, and created databases of shrimp populations and habitats. Laurette guided them to choose topics for written and oral reports, done in pairs or individually, on a range of topics including habitat loss and human impact on ecosystems, shrimp life cycles, and the conditions shrimp need in order to thrive. Committees were formed to be in charge of fundraising (which included, of course, bake sales), designing and marketing t-shirts, publishing a regular newsletter, and creating a public relations campaign. The effort to save the shrimp became the class theme that inspired their learning in several integrated subject areas for an entire year.

From scientific papers written by the California Department of Fish and Game, the class learned that Stemple Creek, a shrimp habitat not far away, was classified as "degraded" due to ranching activity. Students called a rancher, who agreed—after some persuasion—to allow access to his property, where the creek was almost bare of vegetation and eroded along its banks by cattle. Laurette contacted a professional restoration firm, Prunuske Chatham, Inc., whose experts trained the students on how to properly conduct a restoration effort. Students also contacted experts from various local and state government agencies and organizations such as the Audubon Society, the Nature Conservancy, and the Coastal Conservancy.

In the classroom, students improved their reading skills, especially for non-fiction text because of all the research they were doing and the real-world documents they examined. They were motivated to work on their writing skills as they composed letters and articles for the newsletter, learning how to structure an essay with an introduction, supporting evidence, and conclusion. They learned to use persuasive language as they created public relations materials. The class kept a growing vocabulary word list, which included terms from science and social studies and concepts such as interdependence, government regulation, and native vs. invasive plant and animal species.

In March, the class donned their boots, grabbed their shovels, and made the first of several trips to the ranch to dig holes for willows and other native plants, clear obstructions, and shore up the banks of the creek. By then they had also been talking with local newspaper and television reporters, called and written letters to politicians, and made presentations in public forums and at a legislative hearing in the state capitol in Sacramento. Their work continued over the spring, including occasional Saturdays and even over the summer — and other students and teachers have followed in their footsteps for many years since then.

Reflections on the Project

As a result of this project Laurette's students gained a lot more than knowledge of basic science, although they learned plenty about ecosystems, food chains, producers and consumers, and how plants and animals survive by adapting to their environment. By focusing on a real-world issue and actively working to save a species, students were motivated to use reading and writing skills, apply math, learn geography, and use their artistic and design talents. They had multiple opportunities to practice success skills such as collaboration, project management, oral presentation, and systems thinking. For example, in addition to ecosystems in nature the students understood more about how local and state governments, along with non-governmental organizations, worked as a system to deal with issues of land use and environmental protection. And the students became better thinkers, as they learned to analyze data, make evidence-based arguments, and solve problems big and small.

The children learned how to be persistent, assertive, and persuasively communicate with adults—and gained confidence that would stay with them as they grew up, as many students told Laurette later. The project provided a highly effective form of career education, too, as the 10-year-olds saw adults working in various roles and settings. And perhaps most important, these young people learned they could make a difference as capable, committed citizens. As one student put it, "I never expected this to happen, and I feel like we've done a lot. I think this project changed everything I thought we could do. I always thought kids meant nothing, but it showed me that kids can make a difference in the world, and that we are not just little dots."

Looking back, Laurette comments:

"One thing I always tried to do was to show the balance between environmental protection and economic concerns that affect real people, to teach students that issues like this aren't easy, one-sided or simplistic. I wanted them to respect all points of view and to think for themselves. This kind of project allows you to find out about yourself, to test who you are as a person, because you're not just following directions."

Project #6: Selling a Cell

THE PROJECT IN BRIEF

Project Title: Selling a Cell

Project Author: Gina DeLorenzo, White Hall Elementary School, Fairmont, WV

Content Area: Math (pre-Algebra)

Grade Level: 5th

Duration: 2 weeks; approximately 45 minutes per day, 5 days a week

Driving Question: Which cell phone service plan best meets the needs of my family?

Project Summary: Students are asked to compare cell phone service plans and choose an appropriate plan for their family's needs. In teams, students conduct research on cell phone use that includes parent interviews, peer surveys, and analysis of various service plans and present their findings to the class. Individual students then create a slide presentations for an audience of parents, peers, and adults from the school, to explain which service plan they recommend for their family and why.

Major Student Products: Graph comparing cell phone service plans; slide presentation by teams of survey data analysis; slide presentation by individuals of recommended cell phone service plan.

For More Information: This project may be found in the West Virginia Department of Education project library at **wvde.state.wv.us/teach21/pbl.html**. (Several similar projects may be found by searching online project libraries and websites.)

How the Project Was Conceived and Planned

Gina wanted to find an engaging way to teach 5th grade math standards for pre-algebra, including "demonstrate understanding of patterns, relations, and functions," and plotting points on a coordinate plane. Another standard she wanted to teach was the concept of "collecting, displaying, and analyzing data in a variety of ways."

Driving Question: Which cell phone service plan best meets the needs of my family?

The idea for a project came when one of her students, a boy whose birthday was approaching, asked the class for ideas for how to convince his parents to get him a cell phone. Hearing the students' lively interaction, Gina quickly realized how relevant and important cell phones were to today's students. She decided to craft a challenging problem-solving project involving the analysis of competing cell phone plans. The topic would definitely create in her students the "need to know" her math content objectives. There would also be opportunities to build students' reading skills, specifically in comprehending informational/technical text.

How the Project Was Managed

Gina launched the project by sharing the following problem-solving scenario with her class:

> "Your parents' cell phone service contract is about to expire. Your birthday is fast approaching and you feel it is the perfect opportunity to ask for a cell phone. Your parents have agreed to consider this purchase and add you to their plan. However, they need you to investigate what service plans are available. They are willing to contribute $50.00 toward a cell phone which includes start up fees, and an additional $20.00 more per month on the new contract. You are to evaluate each plan and make a presentation to your parents with your recommendation."

Coached by Gina, the class had a discussion to analyze the task they had been given, creating a list of questions under the heading "What do we need to know?" Among these were, "How many service plans are there and how are they different?" "Which plans are most popular?" "Which plan is the cheapest?" and "How many minutes per month would we need?" The students were curious about the topic and eager to start the project.

After explaining some of the project's details — the team and individual products to be completed, the project calendar, and the format of presentations — Gina put the students into teams of four students. She got them started on their first team task: surveying their peers to find out the average number of minutes and text messages used per month. Gina showed them how to do it with an example on the board, then each team created survey questions and a system for recording responses. Over the next two days they conducted their surveys, then summarized and analyzed the data. The first individual task was for students to find out what cell phone services and plans were used at home. In teams, they developed and agreed on good interview questions for their parents. When each student returned with their answers in two days, this data was factored into the team's considerations. Each team created PowerPoint slides to display their survey and interview data and made a brief presentation to the class at the end of the first week.

On the second day of the first week, each team began analyzing cell phone service plans by going to various service provider websites and reading about what was offered. Gina provided a note-taking guide as a scaffold for finding key information on the sites. The students had more questions after two days of this, which they wrote up in preparation for visits to the classroom by employees from two local cellular telephone service companies. The students also used the interactive Q & A feature found on some of the websites to find answers to their questions.

On the third and fourth days Gina began a series of math lessons that would continue into the following week. For example, she taught her students how to make sense of the different rate plans and plot the data on a graph. She showed how the x-axis should be labeled with the number of minutes and the y-axis is labeled with cost, the dependent variable. Students wrote entries in a math journal to explain what they were finding in various service plans and reflect on their progress, so Gina could help those who needed it. She also used short written exercises to check for each student's understanding of the math.

The second week focused on how individual students could apply what they were learning to their own family's situation. Each student stayed with his or her team so they could ask each other questions, compare ideas, and co-create slides to present at the end of the week. To guide the students, Gina showed them the rubric she would use to assess their slides and five-minute presentations. They practiced presentations in their teams on Thursday and used the rubric to assess themselves.

On Friday afternoon the parents arrived in the classroom. After an orientation to the project they moved to one of four locations Gina had set up for presentations: her room, the cafeteria, the library, and the computer room. Monitoring the other rooms were the principal, another teacher, and the librarian, who Gina had coached on the format, timing, and use of the rubric. Also attending were the two guest speakers from the cell phone companies, who were asked not to do any "sales" work if they asked students any questions. Gina was curious to hear their assessment of how well her students understood and explained the details about service plans (they were generally impressed, they later reported). Students in each room who were not presenting watched and listened and marked a rubric as they assessed each of their peers.

Reflecting on the Project

According to Gina, the project "took on a life of its own." Her students were thoroughly engaged and took ownership of their team work as well as their individual presentations. They appreciated the opportunity to actively explore a topic relevant to their own lives as they did research, interviewed their parents, analyzed information, and drew conclusions supported by evidence.

They learned math skills more thoroughly because they had to apply them, Gina noted, compared to how she used to teach the same material, and she was able to cover the same amount.

 Gina was happy to see a real effect of the project:

"After completing the project, some students used the information they had gathered and actually persuaded their parents to change the cell phone plans they were using."

Project #7: What's With This Guy?

THE PROJECT IN BRIEF

Project Title: What's With This Guy?

Project Author: Aaron Eisberg, Napa Valley Unified School District, CA

Content Area: Science (Biology, human anatomy)

Grade Level: 5th

Duration: 2 weeks; approximately 45 minutes per day, 5 days a week

Driving Question: How can we diagnose a sick patient and recommend the best treatment?

Project Summary: Students playing the role of medical school students gather information from a patient who describes symptoms that lead them to suspect a problem with the circulatory or respiratory system. After lessons in which they learn about these systems, students work in teams to research additional information on the Internet so they can make a preliminary diagnosis. They decide what additional information they would need in order to be sure of their diagnosis, then present their analysis and conclusions to a panel of adults in the role of medical school professors.

Major Student Products: Oral presentation with PowerPoint slides.

For More Information: Contact Aaron Eisberg, Napa Valley Unified School District, CA at **aesiberg@nvusd.k12. ca.us.**

How the Project Was Conceived and Planned

In previous years, Aaron Eisberg had taught the circulatory system in the human body through a series of activities that were standards-based, but somewhat disconnected and lacking in relevance. For example, students cut out pieces of a paper model of the heart and pasted them together to demonstrate their knowledge of its structure. This approach produced short-term success on a unit test, but two weeks afterward, the students had forgotten most of what they had learned. Aaron also felt that students were bored with the usual note-taking and cutting and pasting and that the process did not meet the needs of his diverse group of students. They wanted something more engaging, relevant and challenging.

Driving Question: How can we diagnose a sick patient and recommend the best treatment?

Aaron talked with a local doctor who provided insights about how science concepts and critical thinking skills are used in the medical field. Together they designed a project that would present students with a challenging problem — a patient describing a list of symptoms — and have the students diagnose the cause and recommend a treatment plan. (A similar method of instruction, the form of PBL known as problem-based learning, is used in many medical schools.) Aaron hoped that this real-world inquiry and culminating presentation to a panel, which included a teacher, school administrator, and health care worker, would produce higher levels of engagement and successful in-depth learning. To address additional science content standards, Aaron decided to construct the scenario in a way that also made an illness in the respiratory system possible. That way, students would need to know about both the circulatory and respiratory systems in order to diagnose the patient.

How the Project Was Managed

Aaron launched the project by telling students that they would be learning about the human body by playing the role of students in medical school who are learning how to diagnose and treat a patient. They were going to present their analysis and recommendations in two weeks to their professors. Aaron told his students they were going to start with a role-play scenario in which he would be playing Howard, a young man with a medical condition, and they were going to ask him questions. Before "Howard" arrived, Aaron put students in teams of three to plan their questions, then left the room. He sauntered into the room a minute later, playing his role as a cool character who had been "made to come in" by his girlfriend, took a seat, and waited for the students to ask him their questions. He answered briefly and reluctantly, revealing that he was short of breath, fatigued, felt abdominal pain, and had a rapid heart rate. Apart from describing these four symptoms, he made sure his answers to questions were vague so the students would have little else to go on for now.

After there were no more questions to ask "Howard," he left the room and Aaron led the students in a discussion of what they knew about the problem so far and what they needed to know. They created a list of questions on chart paper, on everything from what causes these symptoms, to what parts of the body could be affected, to what Howard's lifestyle was. This "need to know list" became the class's road map for the series of lessons and research that followed over the next two weeks.

Each day, the teams took one item from the "need to know" list and gathered information on the topic by searching the Internet. Students had to prove that their information was accurate by identifying three to four Web resources that provided the same information. Aaron felt that the key to the success of the project was teaching research skills and how to differentiate between relevant and non-relevant information. He reviewed the students' daily journal entries about what they were learning to keep up on their progress, address any issues, and redirect teams if necessary. He also provided some print resources and conducted lessons, drawing from the need to know list, on the circulatory and respiratory systems, blood, and the major organs in the human body. As students learned more about what conditions could be causing Howard's symptoms, they added more questions to the need to know list and crossed off the ones they had answered.

The class decided they would have to find out more information from Howard. Each team made suggestions and the class agreed on a written form for him to fill out, giving his medical history and answering further questions about his symptoms. Aaron provided Howard's answers the next day of project work, and soon the "med students" were narrowing down the possibilities to conditions such as asthma, cystic fibrosis, and sickle-cell anemia. Each team began planning their presentation, in which they had 10 minutes to explain their hypothesis about Howard's problem. The teams had to begin by describing the organ systems in the body that might be affected, and conclude by stating what further information they might need in order to be more certain about their diagnosis.

On the day of presentations, each team showed PowerPoint slides and explained their analysis to a panel that included Aaron, a doctor invited as a guest, and the school principal. The panelists asked challenging questions but the students handled it smoothly and confidently. Each student also took an individual test on the science content.

Reflecting on the Project

After the project, Aaron saw its value compared to how he used to teach the same material. His previous units on the circulatory and respiratory systems and human anatomy, even though they did have some hands-on activities, worked well only for short-term memory of facts. He noted, "After I shaped the unit into a project, I learned that real-world application results in much deeper understanding and retention of concepts." As they reflected on the project, his students commented that they improved their ability to work with their peers and problem-solve. They also loved the opportunity to see how doctors use knowledge and inquiry skills to diagnose their patients. And they had fun while they learned.

 Aaron reports that the project's momentum continued:

"*After the project was over, students were still interested in the topic, so we continued with an inquiry into student lifestyles, which was aligned with the health curriculum. They learned how altering a lifestyle can reduce the chances of getting, or minimize the effects of, heart and lung diseases.*"

Index

A

assessment, 47-52
  of collaboration, 48-49
  of communication (oral presentation), 50-51
  of content knowledge, 48-49
  of critical thinking, 49-51, 112, 117
  during presentations, 112
  formative, 104-108
  of individual students, 34
  of success skills, 49-52, 112, 117
  self, 105, 115-117
  with rubrics, 51-52
audiences for project presentations, 36-37, 108-112

B

Berger, Ron, 104, 107
Bloom's taxonomy, new, 99
books about PBL, 123

C

calendar for projects, 64-66
  example calendar, 150-151
  form, 130-131
celebrating success, 114-115
checkpoints, 64-66, 104-108
classroom set up for PBL, 87
collaboration
  assessing skills, 49-52
  building skills, 93-96
  definition, 31
  establishing criteria for, 94
  managing student teams, 93-98
  modeling skills, 96
  rubrics for, 134-135
Common Core State Standards
  English Language Arts: presentation skills, 32
  technology in, 55
communication skills, 30-31
  assessing presentation skills, 49-52
  definition, 31
contracts, for student teams, 95
  example contracts, 138-139

concepts, as a focus for projects, 30, 42
critical thinking/problem solving
  assessing skills, 49-50
  definition, 31
  in student-friendly language, 100
  modeling, 101-102
  teaching, 98-103
  websites for, 103
critique protocol, for products, 107
culture of inquiry, 86-87
curriculum mapping, 30
  example map, 152-153

D

daily teaching and learning tasks, 63-66
data, to plan re-teaching and improve projects, 120-121
definition of PBL, 5-7
Driving Question, 37-42
  examples of, 39-41
  purpose and characteristics of, 37-38
  reflecting on it during project, 97
  template for, 39
  types of, 38-41

E

effectiveness of PBL, 12-13
elementary school programs and PBL, 14-15
English Learners, 11-12
Entry Document sample, 62, 76
Entry Events, 59-62
Essential Project Design Elements, 7, 20-21
experts, working with, 66

F

fishbowl modeling of collaboration skills, 96
first project advice, 28
flow of a project diagram, 46
formative assessment, 104-108

G

Gold Standard PBL, 7, 20-21
groups, see teams